Studies in applied regional science

This series in applied regional, urban and environmental analysis aims to provide regional scientists with a set of adequate tools for empirical regional analysis and for practical regional planning problems. The major emphasis in this series will be upon the applicability of theories and methods in the field of regional science; these will be presented in a form which can be readily used by practitioners. Both new applications of existing knowledge and newly developed ideas will be published in the series.

Studies in applied regional science
Vol. 7

Production systems and hierarchies of centres

The relationship between spatial and economic structures

Jan Gunnarsson
University of Gothenburg

Martinus Nijhoff Social Sciences Division
Leiden 1977

ISBN 90 207 0688 8

Photoset in Malta by Interprint (Malta) Ltd.

Printed in the Netherlands by Intercontinental Graphics Dordrecht

Preface

The ideas of this book originate from a research group at the Department of Economics in Gothenburg working with the problem of "Relations between Physical and Economic Planning".The research was financed by grants from the Swedish Council for Building Research.

Among all the persons, who from time to time were associated to the project group, the author wishes to express his particular thanks to Ph.D. Rune Jungen, Ph.D.Johan Lönnroth and M.A.Lars Andersson.

This book is also my doctoral dissertation for which professor Åke E. Andersson has acted as supervisor. It has been a privilege for me to have him as my supervisor. I have benefited a great deal from a professional as well as a personal point of view.

There are other members of the Department of Economics to whom I am indebted. Professor Harald Dickson was a close reader of my last drafts. The help I got from Ph.D.Lennart Hjalmarsson and Ph.D.Olle Ohlsson has also been indispensable to me.

Ph.D.Barbro Atlestam, M.A.Gösta Olavi and Ph.D.Folke Snickars have assisted with calculations and the solution of mathematical problems. At last the author wishes to thank M.A.Mette Lembring who made the translation from Swedish.

Jan Gunnarsson

Contents

1. Definition of the problem and results

1.1. SOME COMMENTS ON THE STRUCTURE OF SYSTEMS OF CENTRES

The present study discusses characteristics of hierarchy in systems of centres. How is it that in advanced economies a great number of small centres are provided with decentralized service functions: shops, workshops, comprehensive schools, and so on? How is it that these activities also exist in all larger centres and that new ones are added at every level? Size distribution is another characteristic. Why do we have a large number of small towns, a smaller number that are medium-sized and only a few large cities?

Geographers usually order centres in a ranking list. The observed size distribution of towns has usually been fitted to some distribution function, for example, the Pareto, or the log-normal distribution. This structure is so common that it has been recognized in countries with different economic systems as well as in countries at different levels of development (Clark, 1967, p. 317).

Hierarchies of size have not been observed for towns only. Observations of plant sizes have also been fitted to skewed distribution functions (see, for example, Hjalmarsson, 1974). In general, the x per cent largest firms will control more than x per cent of the activity. This structure seems to be general, which is a matter discussed in a comparative study of different economic systems (Engwall 1972). Engwall finds similarities between the size distributions in socialist and capitalist countries.

Two questions may be asked in relation to the above: Firstly, on causality: Is it possible to explain space, considered as a size-ordered system, starting out from systematically operating factors, and are these factors general, in the sense that they also explain the size distribution of plant sizes? Secondly, a normative question:

Is there a distribution that is particularly favourable, and do the conditions for attaining it vary between different economic systems?

Hierarchies of centres have usually been represented on the basis of a parameter (q) of the Pareto distribution.[1] Table 1.1 shows estimations of (q) in a certain number of countries. The estimations, valid for the beginning of the 1950's, have been divided into three groups of countries. In addition, the table presents a group where broadly defined urban areas constitute the geographical base units. In countries with a high value of (q) the size distribution is more even than in countries with a low value.

To judge from the table there is no noticeable difference between socialist and capitalist countries. In developing countries, however, the distribution seems to be more skewed than in other countries. Low values for developing countries can be ascribed to the fact that these countries are characterized by great regional differences in

Table 1.1. The parameter (q) of the Pareto distribution. The values apply to hierarchies of centres.

Countries of Western Europe		Socialist Countries	
Belgium	1.41	Yugoslavia	1.03
Denmark	0.89	Poland	1.09
Finland	1.21	Soviet Union	1.00
France	1.23	Czechoslovakia	1.30
Italy	1.41	Hungary	1.32
Luxemburg	1.11		
Portugal	1.43	*Observations based on broadly defined urban areas:*	
Switzerland	0.61	England	0.98
Spain	1.17	Holland	0.94
Western Germany	1.13	Ireland	1.15
		Iceland	0.91
Developing countries		Norway	0.85
Algeria	0.88		
Argentina	0.91		
Chile	0.91		
Egypt	1.77		
Iraq	0.93		
Pakistan	0.98		
Turkey	1.27		

Source: Richardson, 1973a, p. 162.

income and job opportunities. In consequence, there is a strong immigration to one, or a few, large cities.

The value of (q) seems to be sensitive to how the geographical base unit is chosen. Table 1.1 shows that hierarchies based on broadly defined urban areas usually have lower values for (q). Therefore regional systems seem to be more skewed than systems where cities constitute the units. On the other hand, a relatively high value of q (1.39) has been estimated for the Swedish Labour Market Regions (Andersson et al., 1970, p. 189).

The observed distributions are not exactly log-linear. Allen (1954) shows, for example, that the Pareto distribution in general overestimates the number of small centres, but that it offers a good approximation for towns above a certain size (2000 inhabitants). Advanced economies, with a past as Great Powers, as well as societies with a short period of urbanization, usually have hierarchies of centres where the position of the capital is strong. For such countries the Pareto distribution overestimates the number of centres in the upper size classes (Zipf, 1949), (Clark, 1967, p. 317). Developing countries mostly have a non-linear relationship (Bos, 1965, p. 6).

Neither are observed distributions of plants exactly log-linear. In Norway, Wedervang (1964, p. 83) has found that the largest plants are too small in relation to the Pareto distribution. According to Wedervang, the explanation of this phenomenon is that growth capacity decreases when plants increase in size.

There is probably a certain correspondence between the hierarchies of plants and those of centres in a country. For the upper tail of the city size distribution Edel (1972) has, for example, found that the size of firms is correlated with city size. A general model should therefore combine assumptions in theories of plant distribution with assumptions in spatial equilibrium models. Hjalmarsson (1974) discusses distributions of plants setting out from a production model with economies of scale. Economies of scale also occur in models for hierarchies in systems of centres (Tinbergen, 1967a). Besides economies of scale, Tinbergen's model contains assumptions on transportation costs and on the existence of an agricultural population spread over a given area.

For each sector, the number of plants is determined on the basis of a given sector output and a given size of plant. The latter is assumed by Tinbergen to be optimal. Plants are combined to centres on the basis of the ranking of sectors: sectors with a great number of plants have a low rank and vice versa. Bakeries, shops and repair workshops, which are numerous, are assigned to the smallest centres but should also exist in all larger centres. Activities such as the building industry, with somewhat fewer units, should not occur in centres smaller than medium-sized towns, whereas the printing industry, which has a small number of production units, only exists in the largest cities. In this way, a system of centres is built up, where there are as many centre ranks as there are sector ranks and where a centre of rank h' is assumed to contain all sectors for which $h \leq h'$.

If the highest-ranking sector in a centre only has one plant and if the number of plants for the sectors is known, Tinbergen shows how to determine the number of centres for each rank.

Tinbergen also indicates formulas for determining the size of centres. When the distribution of plant sizes is given, the model determines a corresponding distribution of centres.

If plants are numerous, centres are numerous too. If plants are few, centres are few. In the first case, transportation costs are high, and in the latter case economies of scale are important compared to transportation costs.

The second question above was if there is any particularly favourable distribution of centres and plants. The normative problem may be treated by starting out from the ratio between the number of centres in one rank and the corresponding number in the next highest rank. The ratio gives an approximation of the average number of satellite towns of a city. It may then be asked whether there is an optimal ratio, that is, a ratio indicating the weighting of economies of scales and transportation costs that is the most advantageous.

The problem is illustrated in figure 1.1 where Tinbergen's model has been used.[2] Distributions of centres and plants have been determined for a tentative ratio of one to four, the value indicated as optimal by Tinbergen (Mennes et al., 1969, p. 224). The distributions determined by the model agree well with the log-linear relationship of the Pareto distribution. If there is an optimal ratio, the model thus determines optimal distributions of plants and centres for given total sector outputs and a known number of sector and centre ranks.

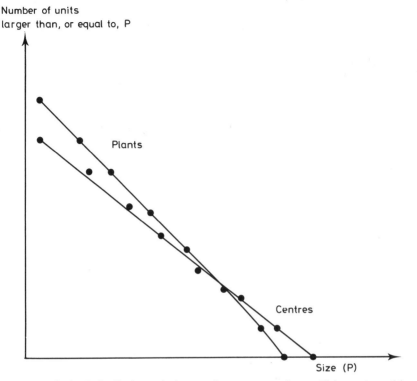

Figure 1.1. Optimal distributions of plants and centres according to Tinbergen's model. Linear logarithmic scale.

1.2. A BRIEF SURVEY OF PROBLEMS

Tinbergen's model, and the extension of his model as elaborated by Bos (1965), constitute the starting-point of our investigation. Figure 1.1 showed that the model generates size distributions of plants and centres which correspond to distributions that have been observed. Since this is also true for other models it is doubtful whether similarity to real distributions can be accepted as proof that the model is 'good'.[3] However, Tinbergen's model has the advantage that it takes into account the determinants that the distributions of plants and centres have in common. This will be dealt with further in chapter 5.

Not only centre sizes, but also activities, are ordered in a regular way within the system of centres. The ordering of activities, or sectors, can be done on the basis of a distance criterion, as in the model discussed by Mennes et al. (1969, p. 269). In this case the distance criterion not only includes transportation costs, in the narrow sense of the word, but also cultural and institutional barriers to spatial mobility. Commodity groups are assumed to be ranked according to the size of the market area. For an arbitrary geographical unit, whose size is equal to that of the market area for commodities of rank h, the model implies that all commodities of rank $\leq$ h are produced within the unit. Commodities of rank > h are imported, which requires that at least some commodity of rank > h is produced within the unit and exported in order to finance import. This type of model has been used, for example, to study integration effects in development planning (Mennes, 1973). Generally, the starting point has been a rough ranking of sectors into international, national and regional.

In hierarchies of centres, indivisibilities are added as an important explanatory factor.[4] Mennes et al. do not specify indivisibilities in their model, which makes it less interesting to the present study.

The impact of indivisibilities on the system of centres is evident in a macro-perspective. This stands out clearly when all activities are dealt with simultaneously and when markets and population are not considered as located. If possibilities for agricultural were about equal everywhere, and if natural resources were uniformly available, the most economic solution, assuming complete divisibility, would be an even distribution of all activities. On every square kilometer the "commodity basket" produced would be exactly the same, and the level of an economic activity would not vary from one place to another. It is only when indivisibilities are introduced that the problem of agglomeration can be explained.

The "plant" is assumed to be indivisible. All forms of economies of scale are classified as "indivisibilities", as in the studies of Kaldor (1934) and Koopmans (1957).[5] Three types of economies of scale are usually mentioned in the literature. The first of these is determined mainly by the law of nature. If, for example, the diameter of a pipe-line is doubled, the capacity quadruples, whereas costs only double. The second type concerns efficiency in the combination of production factors. A third form of economies of scale is considered to result from the increased specialization made possible by an increase in the scale of production. Silberston (1972) presents a more detailed classification of economies of scale.

Indivisibilities are important in Tinbergen's model. Transportations are impossible without costs, but Tinbergen simplifies by not indicating these costs in the model. Instead plants are combined to optimal systems of centres (that is, with minimized transportation costs), based on the number of plants that are necessary for the sectors in order to satisfy a given demand. The size of the plant is assumed given and optimal.

Thus sectors are usually ordered in space according either to a distance criterion, or else with respect to a criterion of indivisibility. In both cases it is a question of approximations, motivated by the difficulty of inserting transportation costs into those general models where economies of scale also occur. The last chapter discusses a model where systems of centres and plant capacities are determined within the same programming model. Both economies of scale and transportation costs occur in the model. Within this model optimal distributions of centres and plants are simultaneously determined.

Chapters 4 and 5 discuss characteristics of systems of centres that are optimal with regard to production and transportation costs. This criterion can be criticized for being far too restricted. However, the present study shows that a system of centres with minimized transportation costs can have characteristics which make the use of this system advantageous during the micro-phase of Tinbergen's method for stepwise planning (Tinbergen, 1967b). To our knowledge, this linking-up to a specific method of planning has never before been presented as clearly (see 2.2.3).

Characteristics of optimal systems of centres have been treated among others by Bos (1965) and Tinbergen (1967a). Systems were then determined for alternative criteria of transportation costs. In the present study determinations of optimal systems of centres are carried out. These are different from those of Tinbergen and Bos in so far as we take an interest in the importance to optimum of the location of natural resources and the value of a coefficient relating final demand for agricultural products to total income.

The models presented here are a development of those of Tinbergen and Bos in that they include the production of intermediate products (input-output coefficients). Bos (1965, p. 67) has a programming model, though it is solely constructed with regard to vertically integrated industries. Neither does Bos use any algorithm to solve programming problems which contain integer variables, and for this reason important parts of the system of centres must be given a priori. In one of our calculations, an algorithm for combinatorial solution of integer problems (OPHELIE MIXTE) is used. This solution is consequently less a priori than Bos's solution.

Both Tinbergen and Bos assume that plant capacities are given. The same assumption is also made in the first model of this study, but in the model presented in chapter 5, both plant capacities and the system of centres are endogenously determined.

What is most interesting to present problems of regional politics is probably not the state of a population and housing structure. The debate on regional problems has instead been all the more taken up with geographical mobility. However, a static model, like ours, can also be useful for studies of changes over time. The assumptions of the model can be modified and the corresponding deviations may be interpreted as an evolution over a certain span of time. How this can be done is illustrated by our calculations.

One of our hypotheses is that decentralized decisions based on price information generate more activities in the largest centres than what is optimal with respect to transportation costs. If this hypothesis proves correct, the conclusion must be that an optimally decentralized geographical structure presupposes other systems of implementation.[6] More precisely the question posed is whether the optimal solution can be maintained when decision-making is individual and based on price information. Our analysis shows that the model with given plant capacities gives the same results as those of Serck-Hanssen (1970, p. 96). He shows that some sectors must be taxed in such centres where they should not have any plant. We show, however, that Serck-Hanssen's conclusion has probably to be modified when fixed costs are also taken into consideration. This problem is further developed in our second model where variations in investment costs are indicated.

Ever since the classic article of Koopmans and Beckman (1957), the question of whether there is a price consistent with optimum has mainly concerned the role of indivisibilities in this context. With our second model we demonstrate that characteristics of dependency between activities are also decisive in the search for a price system.

1.3. SUMMARY AND MAIN CONCLUSIONS

Chapter 2 treats theories aimed at explaining the hierarchy of systems of centres. In some cases the size distribution of centres has been determined on the basis of stochastic models. One weakness in the stochastic model is that only size is explained, omitting the composition of individual centres. The scope of the problem is thus more limited than in this study. We therefore link up to the tradition of Christaller, Lösch and Tinbergen, who also discuss the composition of centres and relationship between centres. The hierarchical characteristics of these models are based on three conditions, which are to be found in Bos (1965, p. 89). They are:

1. Agricultural production and population are spread over a given area.
2. The production of non-agricultural industries is characterized by indivisibilities leading to economies of scale.
3. Transports of goods and services give rise to transportation costs.

The models of Christaller, Lösch and Tinbergen leave out the production of intermediate products. Among the existing extensions which also consider input-output coefficients, those of Lefeber (1958) and Bos (1965) will be discussed here. Lefeber's model lacks indivisibilities and thus excludes one of Bos's conditions for hierarchy. Consequently, Lefeber's work is not a hierarchy model. As it is classic, however, the model is included. Lefeber was the first to systematically discuss problems of dependencies in spatial models. Even so, the model has sometimes been criticized for its assumptions concerning dependencies. It lacks, among other things, a connection between the use of a factor stock and the needs of this stock for input of goods. This connection is missing because Lefeber distinguishes special consumption activities. It is evident that Lefeber primarily refers to labour force when he speaks of factor stock. But, in our opinion, the means of subsistence required by the labour force should be regarded as equivalent to other inputs in the process of production. This demand is only satisfied if there is a feedback between production and consumption.

The work of Bos (1965, p. 80) is an extension of the hierarchy model of Tinbergen where input-output coefficients occur. There is no factor stock. Neither does Bos distinguish any special activities of consumption, but the necessaries for the workers and their families enter directly into the process of production. The weakness of Bos's model is that it assumes a method for the ranking of sectors. The method used by Bos is based on implicit transportation costs and on a ranking of sectors according to the number of plants needed to produce given sector outputs. Since the model is not formulated as a grogramming problem, Bos never shows whether the solution found is optimal with regard to transportation costs. Chapter 4 and 5 present two programming models where the ranking of centres and sectors is determined within the models.

Chapter 3 contains an empirical study where component analysis is used to examine the degree of correspondence between the theoretical systems of centres and the Swedish system of centres. Component analysis is used to cluster sectors according to similarity in location. The method also classifies the centres by their industrial composition, that is, centres of the same type have the same industrial composition. One advantage of component analysis referred to by some authors, is that it isolates not only types of centre but also the sector clusters composing the respective types. However, this possibility is limited when data are correlated with several components. This is shown in an appendix to chapter 3, where component analysis is also presented. Since the sector groups occur within several types of centre, such an intercorrelation is inevitable when studying systems of centres. We therefore combine types of centre and sector clusters in a table.

Data refer to 1971. They have been taken from the Swedish Industrial Statistics indicating the distribution of plants among municipal blocks. In total, the material comprises 141 sectors and the 190 largest Swedish municipal blocks. Three components represent important structural characteristics of the Swedish system of centres, distinguishing three hierarchically ordered types of centre. One of them contains the ten largest cities. The second type comprises the next fifty municipal blocks. The third type contains the remaining small centres. At low correlations, the components 4 to 10 have also been investigated. Only small centres are classified by components 4–10, and these types of centre cannot be ranked according to size.

The result should be interpreted with care. Component analysis has the advantage of contributing towards the formulation of hypotheses, but it hardly gives any ready answers. It is nevertheless interesting to establish how well our result agrees with Tinbergen's system of centres. According to this system, the ratio for advanced economies should be one to four between centres of a given rank and those of the next lowest rank. Each metropolitan area is considered as one municipal block. Then our result indicates a distribution of Swedish municipal blocks between three levels according to 10.50.177. A Tinbergen system, based on the number of ten for the class of largest cities, would result in 10.40.160.

When clustering the sectors it was observed that the majority of sectors fell into four groups. One group is strongly represented on all three levels of the system of centres. Two groups are primarily represented only on the two highest levels, whereas the fourth group primarily occurs in the ten largest municipal blocks. A deviation was observed in relation to Tinbergen's system, that is, one sector group is missing in certain centres where the group should theoretically have been represented. Probably this deviation depends on the fact that the Swedish agriculture and forestry are not evenly spread. In Tinbergen's model it is assumed that all natural resources are evenly dispersed in space.

A programming model is presented in chapter 4. The ranking of sectors and centres is determined by the model. Input-output coefficients, indivisibilities and transportation costs are included. The assumptions of dependency are the same as those of Bos. The model has two further characteristics. Firstly, it distinguishes between foot-loose sectors and locationally restricted sectors. Foot-loose sectors and their total sector outputs at different locations are determined by the model. The total outputs of restricted sectors are taken as given for each place. The second characteristic concerns the way of treating indivisibilities. It is thereby assumed that a foot-loose sector has a given plant capacity which has to be exceeded in a centre. This condition is satisfied by an integer variable of either zero or one, depending on whether or not a plant is present in a centre.

The objective function implies that total costs for transportation are minimized. An alternative formulation would be to extend the minimization procedure to investment costs. Such a change in the objective function is, however, only meaningful if the centres have different capital output ratios, and there is no such assumption made. The model assumes a closed economy. Section 4.3 shows that the model can be adjusted in order to include external trade as well.

In 4.4 the model is used for calculations, the purpose of which is to indicate characteristics of systems of centres that are optimal with regard to transportation costs. Similar problems have been treated previously by Bos (1965) and Tinbergen (1967a). Sensitivity analyses have then applied to alternative criteria of transportation costs. We have chosen to focus our attention on the effects of different assumptions concerning the location of natural resources and the structure of production and consumption on the system of centres.

At first this is illustrated in 4.2 by some simple models where it is demonstrated how the number of centres is influenced by the way in which input-output coefficients, coefficients relating final demand to income and ratios between value added and income are related to freight rates for individual commodities. The models are only useful in small and adjusted problems. The sensitivity analysis which builds on the programming model is more general. The programming model is used in three numerical examples. In the first two, total sector outputs are determined in seven centres for four foot-loose sectors, as well as deliveries of goods between the centres. The total outputs of two restricted sectors are given in the centres. The difference between the examples lies in the value of the coefficient relating final demand for agricultural products to total income. The third example is an effort to discover the nature of optimum at different spatial distributions of restricted sectors. Data on input-output coefficients, coefficients relating value added and final demand to income have been collected from the revised version of the Swedish Long Term Surveys for 1970.

In the example with a smaller share for the agricultural sector (the first example), optimum seems to imply that sectors with economies of scale should be concentrated to one centre. This result is similar to actual observations, namely that in advanced economies, (that is, countries where the agricultural sector is small), it is difficult to see whether there are any locally balanced sectors in the largest cities. In the second example (where the share of agriculture is greater), the solution seems to imply a structure of the system of centres that is totally consistent with the system of

Tinbergen. Both examples assume that restricted sectors are evenly distributed among the centres. A subsequent question is then whether a different distribution of the restricted sectors can preclude concentration to one centre even if the agricultural sector is small. This question is studied in the third example, where the share of agriculture is the same as in the first example. The only difference between the examples is that, in the third, a distinction is made between an agricultural region and a region of extractive industry. Under these circumstances the earlier concentration to one centre is replaced by a corresponding concentration to the agricultural region. Within the agricultural region, on the other hand, two geographical levels were obtained with a composition of centres and deliveries of goods that are similar to the hierarchy in Tinbergen's model.

The next question is whether optimum of the model can be maintained when decision-making is individual and based on price information. If this is impossible, one more question is raised, namely what the nature of an alternative system of implementation would be like. Problems of decentralized decision-making are discussed in 4.5, on the basis of the Lagrangean of the model presented in chapter 4. The discussion leads to the conclusion that an optimal system of centres can only be maintained under decentralized decision-making when there is a central planning organ. Such an organ should be aware of the solution to programming model and also perform the following functions:

1. Subsidize restricted sectors in centres where optimum leads to production at the minimum level at which production is feasible in a plant. Such a minimum level is motivated by economics of scale and fixed costs.
2. Tax foot-loose setors in some centres where, according to the optimum, they should not have any plant.
3. Subsidize foot-loose sectors in centres where the optimum leads to production at the minimum level at which production is feasible in a plant, that is, where sector outputs correspond to plant capacities.

Our interest is focused particularly on the need for taxing foot-loose sectors in certain centres. A simplified example shows that the need for such a taxation is particularly strong in the largest cities. Without taxation, and when decision-making is based on price information, large centres have a tendency to contain more activities than what is optimal (with respect to transportation costs). The negative result concerning the price mechanism was obtained without explicit consideration of fixed costs. The section also discusses, however, whether the conclusion concerning the price mechanism has to be modified if such consideration is taken.

In chapter 5 the assumption of given plant capacities is abandoned. Fixed costs and transportation costs are directly minimized in the model, implying that the size and the location of a plant are determined simultaneously. Furthermore, dependencies between sectors (input-output) and economies of scale are taken into consideration. The previous model (in chapter 4) has the weakness that a total concentration to a large centre is only precluded by the fact that locations are given for restricted sectors. The way the objective function is formulated it would therefore be preferable, in the long run, to change the locations of restricted sectors, so as to concentrate all production to one large centre. In chapter 5 the assumption of restricted sectors is abandoned. Concentration is instead prevented by the scarcity of available land in the centres. The fifth chapter is more preliminary than the previous ones. It aims primarily at indicating a possibility for further research.

The fourth chapter discusses the market institution; more specifically the role of prices as informers in allocation decisions. In chapter 5 we return to the importance of the market institution to the system of centres. This time we are concerned with the cost of using the market to allocate resources. Such costs are assumed to influence the size of plants, which in its turn influences the system of centres. When plants (in the sense of 'enterprises') are numerous, the importance of the market as a resource allocator is greater than when plants are few. According to our view, the existence of many small plants is partly explained by the fact that the cost for using the market to allocate resources is small in relation to the cost for allocating resources within a plant. Control and coordination costs are introduced (a more detailed explanation of the concepts is given in 5.2). The first category of costs indicates the use of resources, influenced by the way of managing and controlling the work within a plant. The second category is related to the use of the price mechanism.

Chapter 5.3 presents a model for quadratic optimization. Control and coordination costs are indicated in the objective function, which also includes transportation and investment costs. Systems of centres and plant sizes are determined in order to minimize the objective function. In the convex case it is shown that optimum can be maintained when decision-making is decentralized (based on commodity prices and land rents) only if the control costs are large in relation to economies of scale and coordination costs.

NOTES

1. The Pareto distribution is usually represented as a log-linear relationship between the size of an element in a size hierarchy, and the number of elements that are greater than, or equal to, this element:

$$\log R = \log K - q \log P$$

where P is the size and R the number of elements that are greater than, or equal to, P. K is a constant. If $q = 1$, then K has a value equal to the size of the largest element of the size hierarchy.

2. Tinbergen's model is presented in section 2.2.2. The number of ranks was set at eight, the total outputs of the sectors at 1000, except for agriculture, where production was fixed at 2000. There is only one centre in the type of centre of highest rank and two centres in the next lowest rank. Thereafter the ratio between the number of centres of a given rank and the number of centres of the next lowest rank is one to four.

3. As a rule, a statistical distribution function is consistent with several theories, and conversely, a theory is consistent with several distributions. Richardson (1973b) makes a survey of a dozen different theories on hierarchies of centres. His conclusion is that it is impossible to favour one theory or another on the basis of its prediction, since any one of the observed statistical relationships is compatible with several theories, while many of the individual theories are consistent with more than one of the standard empirical distributions.

4. Indivisibilities and economies of scale are synonymous in this study.

5. Subsequently, the synonyms indivisibilities and economies of scale are used alternately.

6. The structure of centres in socialist countries does not significantly deviate from capitalist market economies (see table 1.1 and Clark, 1967, p. 317). This is probably due to the fact that it is only during recent years that efforts have been made in the Planning Commissions to integrate spatial and economic planning at the national level.

2. Earlier works on systems of centres

2.1. NECESSARY CONDITIONS FOR HIERARCHY

Chapter 2 deals with theories aimed at explaining hierarchies in systems of centres. Regional economics, in contrast, are mostly concerned with geographical differences in income and employment. Our attention is instead focused on the micro-aspect of spatial economy, where economic action delimits the geographical markets in which commodities and people circulate. The micro-aspect shows the division of the market between producers who become quasi-monopolists within a certain geographical area. Christaller (1966), Lösch (1954) and Tinbergen (1967a) base their models of centres on the specific division of the market into market areas.

Other starting-points are also possible.[1] City size distribution, for example, can be determined on the basis of stachastic models. Simon (1955) argues that city size distribution may be regarded as an equilibrium in a stochastic process. One characteristic of the process is that the probability that the next contribution in population will go to a specific town is proportional to city size. Furthermore, growth only begins when cities reach a certain size. There is a specified probability that this will happen during a period of time. Even if the urban population is normally distributed from the start, Simon demonstrates that after a finite number of periods an equilibrium is reached where city sizes are Pareto distributed.

Different explanations are possible. Simon proposes demographic factors, arguing that increment due to birth surplus should be proportional to city size. This may be combined with an assumption that the rural element is important to the economy and that there is a rural-urban migration. It is reasonable to assume that this migration is also proportional to city size.

Simon's assumptions are hardly very realistic for advanced economies, where neither agriculture nor birth surpluses are particularly common. A more satisfactory approach would also include interurban migration. One such approach is discussed by Haran et al. (1973). Growth is here assumed to be proportional to the number of inhabitants in a city, and there is a certain probability that this growth is the result of immigration from other cities.

Ward (1963), too, discusses a model with migrations. Migration is here assumed to be a reaction to labour demand. As with Christaller, Lösch and Tinbergen, the size of the market area is important, though in another way. Changes in labour demand are related to technological change, which is assumed to occur proportionally to the size of a city's market area.

One weakness of the stochastic model is that it only explains the size distribution while the industrial composition of single centres are omitted. This implies a limitation of the problem compared with the present study. For this reason we link up exclusively to the tradition of Christaller, Lösch and Tinbergen, who also discuss the composition of centres, the relations between different types of centres and the spatial economic landscape.

Christaller, Lösch and Tinbergen consider each agglomeration as the centre of a region composed of smaller centres and rural land. Simultaneously, local demand for commodities leads to a position of dependence in relation to higher-ranking centres. The rank, the orientation of production, and deliveries of goods are determined by the division of labour within the entire system. The system of centres forms an entity with characteristics that are incomprehensible if only single elements are considered. The work of Lösch, Christaller and Tinbergen has thus been regarded as a continuation of the general equilibrium theory, as expounded by Walras and Pareto (Isard, 1956, p. 42). The author considers this parallel to be somewhat doubtful, not only because concepts like hierarchy and structure fall outside the theory of general equilibrium, but also because the assumption of perfect competition is basic to the Walras and Pareto models. However, this assumption cannot be maintained when transportation costs exist.

Bos (1965, p. 89) presents three necessary conditions for a hierarchy of centres. By varying the assumption of transportation costs, Bos (p. 46) shows that the conditions are not sufficient for the structure to be as regular as in Tinbergen's model. It appeared that the system of centres is sensitive to changes in data other than those determined by 2–3 below.

The conditions are as follows:

1. Agricultural production and population are spread over a given area.
2. The production of non-agricultural industries is characterized by indivisibilities leading to economies of scale.
3. Transports of goods and services give rise to transportation costs.

These conditions are put forward, though differently emphasized, by Tinbergen, as well as by Christaller and Lösch. The models of Christaller and Lösch are more definitive than those of Tinbergen, but suffer, however, from distinct weaknesses.

A summary of the criticisms is to be found in Isard (1956, p. 48). See also Paelinck and Nijkamp (1975, p. 70).

It is difficult to insert transportation costs into economic models of a more general type. This is why Tinbergen makes a certain number of simplifying assumptions and advances the model as a hypothesis. His hypothesis is that the model, under certain conditions, leads to optimal systems of centres (in the sense that transportation costs are minimized). One simplification is that transportation costs are implicit. The importance of indivisibilities to the formation of a centre stands out more clearly as a given number of plants is combined to centres according to certain rules. It is assumed that the rules imply a minimization of transportation costs. Lösch, however, determined the number of plants and the system of centres simultaneously, taking into consideration both transportation and production costs.

2.2. MODELS FOR VERTICALLY INTEGRATED INDUSTRIES

2.2.1. Christaller and Lösch

Christaller (1966) bases his theory on central places and the surrounding regions that they supply, that is, the countryside and smaller central places. The central place and its complementary region are interdependent and together form an entity. An activity can only exist in a centre if the demand of the hinterland exceeds a certain threshold. The demand of the complementary region determines the composition of the central place. There is also an upper limit for the hinterland, equal to the maximum transportation distance acceptable to the potential buyer.

The surrounding region should preferably be of a circular shape to cut down transportation costs to minimum (Lösch, 1954, p. 110). This solution, however, leaves areas where no goods are available. Only squares, triangles and hexagons make it possible to subdivide a plane into regular polygons. The hexagon is the form closest to the ideal circle (Paelinck and Nijkamp, p. 71). For each good the market is split up like a honeycomb, with one producer in every cell. The honeycombs are placed on top of each other in order to minimize transportation costs. This implies that central places of one rank are placed in the corners of the complementary region of the next highest central place group (figure 2.1).

The figure only describes part of the system. If this is large (with many central places on each level), there is a ratio of approximately three to one between the number of centres of one rank and the corresponding number for the next highest rank.

Christaller has not summed up the problem in a system of equations and consequently does not show if the solution conforms to the general conditions for equilibrium. This is, on the other hand, shown by Lösch (1954). There is, however, one fundamental difference between Lösch and the theory of general equilibrium, as formulated by Pareto and Walras. To them, the assumption of perfect competition is fundamental – a reasonable assumption if one does not take account of spatial influence. It is impossible, however,

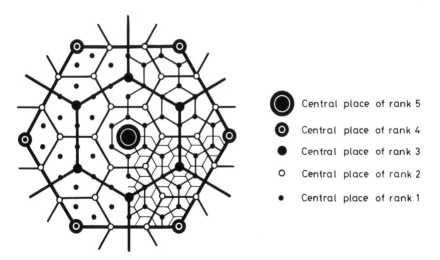

Central place of rank 5
Central place of rank 4
Central place of rank 3
Central place of rank 2
Central place of rank 1

Figure 2.1.

to maintain this assumption when transportation costs are present (Isard, 1956, p. 25). Lösch, on the other hand, links up to the Chamberlin tradition (1938), by assuming an economy working in monopolistic competition.

Thus, Lösch integrates the competition situation into the analysis of spatial structures. The individual firm chooses its location in such a way to achieve the highest profits. The result of this competetive behaviour is a tendency to maximize the number of individual units. Paelinck and Nijkamp (1975 p. 59) maintain that the general location problem, as it is formulated by Lösch, in fact is controlled by two counteracting forces: the maximization of individual profits and the maximization of the number of individual firms.

Lösch makes the following assumptions: Space can be compared to a vast plain where transportation facilities are equal everywhere. Agriculture and natural resources are evenly distributed over the area. The agricultural population and producers of raw material have the same tastes and preferencies. From the beginning every family is self-sufficient. If somebody is capable of producing a surplus, the market of the family expands. But when it is favourable for one family to produce a surplus it is also favourable for others. Competition changes the circular form of the market to a hexagon and the freedom of entry eliminates all profits. Lösch determines the equilibrium of activities located in centres. For each commodity the model determines the price, the number of centres where it is produced and the location of these centres. Five conditions should be fulfilled when all firms are adapted to a situation where there is no incitament to move:

1. Every producer has fixed his location in order to maximize profits.
2. Every good is offered everywhere.
3. All profits are zero.

As long as profits exist, new firms are established. When this happens the demand curve of the single firm swings downwards. Gradually, the market becomes satiated, that is, the demand curve changes till it is tangent to the average cost curve. Profits are then non-existent and no more firms enter the market.

Lösch's fourth and fifth conditions are as follows:

4. A modification in market size should influence average cost and price alike. This is the usual condition for equilibrium in monopolistic competition.
5. For a consumer on the boundary between two market areas, it should be a matter of indifference in which of the two neighbouring centres he makes his purchases.[2]

Lösch's theory of general equilibrium is different from that of Walras in two ways. Firstly, production is divided between several places. Secondly, marginal costs and prices are not equal, as is the characteristic of perfect competition. Lösch replaces the latter by the fourth condition above. The implication of this is that production in a plant does not correspond to a scale where production costs are at mimimum. The actual scale is smaller, so the number of plants will be greater than in the case with perfect competition.

A quality of Lösch's equilibrium is that the number of location of the centres are determined by the model. Herein lies an advantage of Lösch, compared to the attempt in chapters 4–5 where equilibrium is derived from a programming model. As such, the number and location of centres are assumed to be given.

Lösch's structure is different from that of Christaller. They both divide the market into honeycombs. Lösch arranges the honeycombs in a manner in which one centre, the metropolis, contains all commodities, and the honeycombs are turned with the metropolis as axis. Christaller only obtains one principle for the relationship between centres of different sizes, while Lösch obtains three. They are all consistent with minimized transportation costs (see figure 2.2) (Lösch, p. 117). Lösch's system of centres therefore

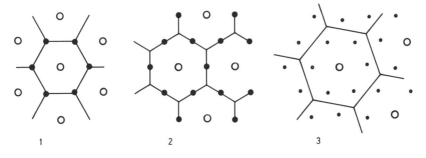

Figure 2.2.

counts three regions with many centres and three with only a few.

Since Lösch presents three possible forms for the market area of a centre, the result of his solution is that centres with identical industrial composition do not always correspond in size. This gives one more difference, compared to the Christaller model, where centres of equal industrial composition are also equal in size. Parr (1973) shows that with four groups of goods the Lösch model gives twenty-six types of centre. Christaller's model would only have given four.

2.2.2. Tinbergen

Tinbergen's model (1967a) is based on a number of simplifications. Transportation costs are, for example, not indicated in the model and the size of plant is taken as given for a sector. Tinbergen, therefore, presents his model as a hypothesis. The hypothesis is that the model, under certain conditions (see below), leads to optimal systems of centres (that is, with minimized transportation costs). As the present work, on the whole, is inspired by the ideas of Tinbergen, his model is presented somewhat more extensively than the two earlier models.

Tinbergen assumes a closed economy, producing the commodities $0, 1, \ldots h \ldots H$ where 0 denotes agriculture. The part of the population occupied in agriculture lives outside the centres and is assumed to be evenly distributed in space. The commodities, agricultural products excluded, are produced in plants of a given capacity. There is a parameter, α_h, for each commodity, indicating its share of the national income, Y. The parameter sum is 1[3]:

$$\sum_{h=0}^{H} \alpha_h = 1$$

As the national income, Y, and the plant capacities, c_h, are assumed known, the number of plants required can be calculated for each commodity. The commodities are ranked according to the size of requirements: The lowest rank is assigned to the commodity calling for the largest number of plants.

The number of plants required in sector h is:

$$n_h = \frac{\alpha_h Y}{c_h} \qquad h = 1, \ldots H$$

where n_h indicates the number of plants.
The ranking is:

$$n_1 > n_2 > \ldots > n_h \ldots > n_H$$

The ranking determines the structure of the system of centres. This includes as many types of centres as there are sector ranks (agriculture excluded), that is, the ranking of centres runs from 1 to H. All production, except agriculture, takes place in centres. The centres are of the same type if they contain sectors of same rank.

Tinbergen's hypothesis consists of three elements:

1. If the highest-ranking sector in a centre is of type h', then this centre also produces all products of types $1 \leq h \leq h'$; the demand for these products within the centre is fully satisfied by production within the centre. Therefore, each type of centre can be characterized by its highest-ranking sector.
2. A centre exports only the products of its highest-ranking sector.
3. Each centre contains only one enterprise of the highest-ranking sector.

Thus, a centre only exports to centres of lower rank and to agriculture. As agriculture does not exist in the centres, these have to import agricultural products from the countryside.

The hypothesis implies that in all centres of type h' all sectors, h, $1 \leq h < h'$ are locally balanced and h' is external. From the hypothesis it also follows that a sector of rank h' exists in all centres of rank $\geq h'$. These sectors are referred to as continuous.

Conditions have been determined which (in some simplified cases) imply that the elements 1, 2 and 3 above lead to minimized transportation costs (Tinbergen, 1967a). Other cases have been studied by Bos (1965, p. 65). He shows that relatively high transportation costs for commodities of low rank mostly lead to a Tinbergen structure as optimum. That high transportation costs probably constitute one of the reasons for the existence of great number of plants in one branch reinforces the credibility of Tinbergen's hypothesis.

Tinbergen determines the income for each type of centre so that exports and imports, for each type, are equal. Thus, the following must hold for agriculture:

$$(1 - \alpha_0)Y^0 = \alpha_0(Y - Y^0)$$

that is

$$Y^0 = \alpha_0 Y$$

Analogously, the income of the lowest-ranking type of centre is:

$$Y^1 = \frac{\alpha_1 \alpha_0 Y}{1 - \alpha_1}$$

The total income of the two groups is

$$Y^0 + Y^1 = \frac{\alpha_0 Y}{1 - \alpha_1}$$

The result may be generalized to

$$\sum_{i=0}^{h} Y^i = \frac{\alpha_0 Y}{1 - \alpha_1 - \ldots - \alpha_h} \qquad h = 1 \ldots H$$

The general expression for the income of type h is

$$Y^h = \frac{\alpha_h \alpha_0 Y}{(1 - \alpha_1 \ldots - \alpha_h)(1 - \alpha_1 - \ldots - \alpha_{h-1})} \qquad h = 1 \ldots H \tag{2.1}$$

The highest-ranking and also exporting sector of a centre only has one plant. The number of centres of rank h may then be written as n_h minus the number of plants for commodity h supposed to cover consumer demand in higher-ranking centres. The number of centres, n^h, is

$$n^h = n_h \frac{\alpha_0}{1 - \alpha_1 - \ldots - \alpha_h} \qquad h = 1 \ldots H \tag{2.2}$$

If (2.1) is divided by (2.2) the average income for a single centre of rank h is

$$\overline{Y^h} = \frac{\alpha_h Y}{(1 - \alpha_1 - \ldots - \alpha_{h-1})n_h} \qquad h = 1 \ldots H$$

2.2.3. Tinbergen's model and the method for stepwise planning

We now elaborate our own viewpoint. To begin with, Tinbergen's system of centres is a 'perfect' hierarchy, while the systems of Christaller and Lösch are examples of two 'quasi'-hierarchies. A precondition for a 'perfect' hierarchy is that sectors are continuous (see definition above), and that the industrial composition of a centre may be divided into local and external sectors. This leads to dependencies between sectors and centres that allow a decomposition of the total system of centres into smaller systems. The market area of an arbitrary centre, h, can be split up into smaller areas and subsystems, where the latter are connected by sectors of rank $\geq h$, but are autonomous with regard to sectors with a lower rank than h (see figure 2.3).

It is true that Christaller's sectors are continuous, but the system is still not a 'perfect' hierarchy, as the centres lack a division between local and external sectors, making the decomposition of the system more complicated than in the Tinbergen case. The greatest deviation from a 'perfect' hierarchy is, however, to be found in Lösch's system, where the sectors are neither continuous nor divided in external and local sectors.

Squares are the only uniform spaces that are consistent with a system of centres, where one market area is completely divisible into a number of areas with stepwise falling rank (the condition for a 'perfect' hierarchy). Systems composed of hexagons, as

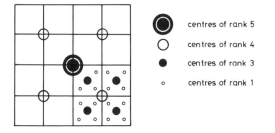

Figure 2. 3. Tinbergen's system of centres – a 'perfect' hierarchy.

those of Christaller and Lösch, for example, do not fulfil these requirements. In contrast, hexagons are more advantageous than squares from the transportation cost point of view. This is the reason why there will always be systems with lower transportation costs than a 'perfect' hierarchy.

Figure 2.3 illustrates Tinbergen's system of centres. The ratio between the number of centres in one group and the number in the next highest-ranking group may be 4, 16, 64 etc. In an advanced economy, Tinbergen argues that 4 would be a reasonable value (Mennes et al., 1969, p. 224).

The space-functional relations of a 'perfect' hierarchy have, amongst other things, a normative interest. We propose to show how a 'perfect' hierarchy is applicable to planning. Since we have used the work of Tinbergen as a starting-point, it is natural to set out from the method for stepwise planning (Tinbergen, 1967b).

The method for stepwise planning consists of three phases: a macro-phase, a middle phase and a micro-phase. During the macro-phase, plans concerning important variables such as income, consumption and investments are elaborated. That is, planning always starts with questions concerning growth and use of natural and energy resources in the future. Incomes agreed to constitute data during the middle phase of planning. During this phase the result from the macro-phase is clarified by a rough division into sectors and regions. During the micro-phase the location of concrete objects is planned. In other words, it is the system of centres and housing that are planned (physical planning). This implies that problems concerning indivisibilities are fundamental during the microphase.

The micro-phase is taken to be based on an investment plan, set up during the middle phase. The following question is asked: In which centres is an expansion, that is, investments in different kinds of sectors, to be carried out when the volume of investments for the single sectors has been determined during the middle phase of the planning? In other words, total output of the sectors constitute the data during the micro-phase.

If Tinbergen's hypothesis about an optimal system of centres is correct, planning during the micro-phase can proceed roughly in the following manner: For each rank, the external sectors of the centres are planned first. When this is done, the planning of local sectors is carried out, independently of what happens in other centres. During the next step, lower-ranking centres are planned. In this way centres within one market area may be planned without regard to the planning in process within other areas on the same geographical level.

The process may be the following: A spatial, unit is divided into four smaller units (see figure 2.3). In the centre of each small unit there is an agglomeration. Only sectors with a small number of plants are located in the first step. The plants should be about as many as the geographical units. The problem of locating production to the four centres is sloved in order to satisfy the requirements for minimized transportation costs. During the next step planning takes place separately within a small unit, divided into four smaller units. Information from the first step is used as data. The location concerns local sectors from the previous step where, in this further division, the number of plants required is the smallest. Should the planning require a further division of local sectors and geographical areas, the procedure is repeated in a third step, and so on.

One important question is the number of geographical levels that are necessary. This probably varies from one country to another, but in the case of Sweden three levels seem reasonable. In any case this could be the conclusion of the study presented in chapter 3.

Mennes (1973) discusses a model suitable for planning during the middle phase. The data of the model consist partly of income targets resulting from the macro-phase, and partly of information about exports and imports for the area. Mennes's optimization criterion implies a minimization of investment outlays. With given restrictions and with such a criterion, consumption is maximized.

The investment plan of the middle phase may be determined by a linear programming model where calculations can be done with known standard methods. The situation during the micro-phase is different. Indivisibilities are here important and therefore the calculations require models for integer and non-linear programming. In chapters 4 and 5 two models are proposed that may be used during the micro-phase.

A system of centres like the one in figure 2.3 has characteristics that can be used in stepwise planning. For this reason it is interesting to test whether the structure is optimal from the transportation cost point of view. This has already been done by Tinbergen (1967a) and Bos (1965, p. 65) with regard to different criteria of transportation costs. In the present study, optimal systems of centres are determined in chapter 4. These numerical examples are different from what has earlier been done by Tinbergen and Bos, in the sense that special attention is given to the sensitivity of optimum to the location of natural resources and the importance of agriculture.

2.3 MODELS WITH INPUT-OUTPUT COEFFICIENTS

There is no production of intermediate goods in the models discussed in 2.2. A more satisfactory approach would be to formulate the hierarchy model considering input-output coefficients. Lefeber (1958) and Bos (1965) are among those who have elaborated the model in this direction.

Lefeber has a transportation sector, that also takes part in the competition for resources. Furthermore, he makes a distinction between activities of production and activities of cunsumption; the latter taking place either on the sites of production or in certain places of consumption. Commodities that are in themselves homogenous are separated if they are consumed in different places. Thus Lefeber derives a transformation curve where each commodity has as many dimensions as there are places of consumption.

When the transformation curve has been derived, a unique and efficient consumption structure is determined for an arbitrary price vector.[4] Every move on the transformation surface implies a reallocation of resources, as well as an influence on the utilisation of inputs in the transportation sector, but the resources are always used efficiently. Lefeber first maximizes the value of consumption at given market prices. Gradually the demand side is also integrated by endogenous determination of prices. In equilibrium the neoclassical relationships between marginal utility and commodity price are fulfilled. The only deviation from Walras is that consumption and production take place at certain locations, connected by a transportation system (Lefeber, 1958, p. 122).

Equilibrium is determined as the optimum of a linear program. For an evaluation of the optimum it is important to know that Lefeber pays no attention to indivisibilities. Thus the model lacks one of the necessary conditions for a hierarchy of centres cited in 2.1. Consequently, Lefeber's work is not a hierarchy model. The reason for including the model is that Lefeber discusses problems of dependencies in spatial models. Even so, the model has been criticized for its simple assumptions of dependency (Å. Andersson et al., 1972). Among other things, it has been said that deliveries between producers are lacking. However, this is also discussed by Lefeber, who argues that the general conclusions are not influenced if input-output coefficients are introduced (Lefeber, 1958, p. 81 and 112). The way Lefeber's model is set up, there is, for example, no connection between the use of existing factor stocks and the need for input of goods to this stock. The lack of such mutual dependencies is due to the fact that Lefeber distinguishes special activities of consumption. It is obvious that Lefeber, by factor stocks, primarily refers to labour (Lefeber, 1958, p. 124). But the means of subsistence required by the workers should, in our opinion, be regarded as equivalent to other inputs in the process of production. This requirement is only fulfilled if there is a feedback between the activities of consumption and production. Even if factor stocks are interpreted as natural resources, feedbacks are necessary. Before sending the raw materials to the production units, they have to be processed and this requires inputs in the form of consumption goods and intermediate products.

Bos's work (1965, p. 80) is an extension of Tinbergen's model where input-output coefficients occur. There is no factor stock. Nor does Bos distinguish any special activities of consumption; but the requirements of the workers and their families enter directly into the process of production. Since Bos also takes indivisibilities into consideration, his work is a hierarchy model.

With input-output coefficients it is not always suitable to determine the system of centres exclusively on the basis of the number of plants needed by the sectors. Bos argues that corrections are necessary, but that they do not change the original formulation of Tinbergen's hypotheses in any decisive way. He finds that sectors which only produce for higher-ranking sectors never find a market outside a centre. Instead the sector occurs exclusively as a locally balanced industry together with receiving sectors. A second result of Bos's is that sectors which only produce for agriculture exist in only one type of centre and are lacking in the others.

SerckHanssen (1961) reaches similar conclusions for industries like dairies and sugar-refineries. These are characterized by economies of scale, in addition to an important demand for agricultural products. Dairies are not therefore present in centres of rank higher than that of the dairies themselves.

Bos starts out from a given ranking of sectors when he sets up his equation system. Besides agricultural, there are three sectors.

The following notations are used:

x^o : total output of agriculture

x_i^h : total output of a sector i located in centre $h = 1, 2, 3$
$i = 1, 2, 3$

a_{ij} : input-output coefficient for deliveries from sector i to sector j

α_i : Coefficient relating final demand for commodity i to income. This includes, for example, the means of subsistence for the workers.

$$\sum_{i=o}^{3} \alpha_i = 1 \text{ must hold}$$

w_j : ratio between value added and output for sector j.

Some relationships are defined:

$$w_j = 1 - \sum_{i=o}^{3} a_{ij}$$

Yet another coefficient, β_i, is defined. It denotes the surplus of sector i per output-unit after subtraction of the internal utilization (including the consumption of the workers):

$$\beta_i = 1 - (a_{ii} + \alpha_i w_i)$$

Finally, an expression is defined for the general input-output coefficient, where consumption and other kinds of final demand also enter the process of production:

$$\gamma_{ij} = a_{ij} + \alpha_i w_j$$

Dependencies between sectors and types of centre are summarized in the matrix A:

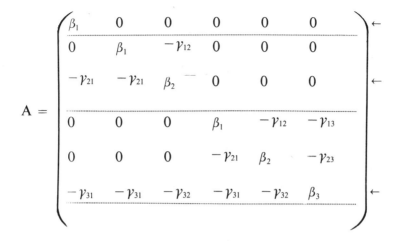

$$A = \begin{pmatrix} \beta_1 & 0 & 0 & 0 & 0 & 0 \\ 0 & \beta_1 & -\gamma_{12} & 0 & 0 & 0 \\ -\gamma_{21} & -\gamma_{21} & \beta_2 & 0 & 0 & 0 \\ 0 & 0 & 0 & \beta_1 & -\gamma_{12} & -\gamma_{13} \\ 0 & 0 & 0 & -\gamma_{21} & \beta_2 & -\gamma_{23} \\ -\gamma_{31} & -\gamma_{31} & -\gamma_{32} & -\gamma_{31} & -\gamma_{32} & \beta_3 \end{pmatrix} \begin{matrix} \leftarrow \\ \\ \leftarrow \\ \\ \\ \leftarrow \end{matrix}$$

The elements between two lines represent the dependencies within one type of centre where the balance of an exporting sector has been marked with an arrow. The lowest-ranking type of centre lacks locally blanced sectors.

Bos's equation system may concisely be written as:

$$Ax = \gamma_{BO} x^\circ \tag{2.3}$$

where the elements in the x-vector represent total output of sectors in the centres, and γ_{BO} the general input-output coefficients for deliveries to the agricultural sector. For the latter vector, the divi-- sion in externally and locally balanced activities implies that the elements 2, 4 and 5 are zero.

If the variables and equations in (2.3) are counted, the system turns out to be indeterminate. It has one variable too much. With the help of the model it is only possible to determine relations between sector groups, while absolute values are determined when one of the variables has been given a value. Even if Bos chooses the agricultural sector, the normative sector may, in principle, be chosen arbitrarily. The choice of the agricultural sector permits, however, an advantageous exploitation of the recursive structure of the model. When the production of agruculture is known, x_1^1 can be determined. In the next step x_1^2 and x_2^2 are calculated; and in the third step x_1^3, x_2^3 and x_3^3.

Bos's model assumes a method for the ranking of sectors. The method used by Bos himself is based on implicit transportation costs and on the ranking of sectors with respect to the number of plants required to produce given outputs of sectors. The model is not formulated as a programming problem, and therefore Bos never shows if the system of centres is optimal with respect to transportation costs.

A programming model is presented in chapter 4. The ranking of sectors and centres is there determined by the model. Input-output coefficients, indivisibilities and transportation costs are indicated in the model. The assumptions of dependency are the same as Bos'. This implies that Lefeber's division between activities of consumption and production are avoided. The assumption is maintained that the number of plants of optimal size is given for a sector. This assumption is abandoned, however, in the model presented in chapter 5.

NOTES

1. For a survey of these, see Richardson (1973b).
2. A formalized presentation of Lösch's equilibrium theory can be found in Isard (1956, p. 45).
3. All prices are constant and 1. The value is equal to quantity for each commodity.
4. There is one, and only one, consumption vector for each price vector. This price vector is tangent to the concave transformation surface.

3. Hierarchy of centres in Sweden at the beginning of the 1970s – an empirical test on Swedish data

3.1. BACKGROUND AND PRESENTATION OF THE PROBLEM

This chapter presents an empirical study of the Swedish system of centres. Our purpose has been to use component analysis to examine whether the structure of the Swedish system of centres resembles the structures of the models in chapter 2. Besides rendering an account of our own study, we present a survey of research made in this field.

Out of the three systems discussed in the preceding chapter we have classified Tinbergen's system as a 'perfect' hierarchy and the systems of Christaller and Lösch as 'quasi'-hierarchies. On the other hand, the systems of Christaller and Tinbergen are similar in the respect that they are both based on continuous sectors. The presence of continuous sectors in the Swedish system of centres is first discussed. The result is expected to reveal the degree of realism in the models of Christaller and Tinbergen, in relation to models where sectors are not continuous as, for example, in Lösch's model. Secondly, the number of centres within each type of centre is determined. This information is utilized to discriminate between Tinbergen's and Christaller's model. The ratio between the number of centres in one type of centre and the number in the next highest rank is three to one in Christaller's model and four to one in Tinbergen's (Mennes et al., 1969, p. 224).

The methodological problem is also discussed. From data about locations, a suitable method should cluster sectors, commodities or activities into a number of homogenous groups. The centres should be clustered according to similarities in composition. One advantage of component analysis sometimes referred to is that it simultaneously determines types of centre and the sector clusters composing these types. Centres are then clustered with respect to component values and sectors with respect to factor loadings.[1] The possibility of stating anything whatsoever about differences between types of centre on the sole basis of component analysis is, however, limited when data are correlated to several components.

Such intercorrelation is common in studies of systems of centres. Comparisons in pairs of factor loadings and component values are therefore unsuitable. Nevertheless, studies of systems of centres exist where such comparisons are made (Berry and Barnum, 1962). A more detailed discussion on this problem is to be found in the supplement to chapter 3, together with a brief presentation of component analysis.

In the introductory chapter it was ·established that the distribution of town sizes is skewed. However, not only population figures are interesting to our investigation but also the composition of the centres with respect to activity structure. There is a limited study of Sweden in 1970 where this composition has been subject to study (Gunnarsson, 1973). Attention was then focused on the employment within the manufacturing industry which takes place in continuous sectors. The concept of continuous sector denoted a sector that, when present in a type of centre of a certain size, also exists in all larger centres.

A sample of 54 centres, distributed among six size groups was used. The following decision rule was applied: if more than one establishment exists in more than half of the selected centres in a size group, the sector belonged to that group. It was shown that out of the selected sectors, which corresponded to the major part of the manufacturing industry, continuous sectors accounted for ca. 80 per cent of employment. On the basis of data from 1950 a similar study has been carried out in Holland (Bos, 1965, p. 9). Sectors were ordered in groups according to the number of production units and centres were ordered according to size. The proportion of activities with few production units was found to increase with the size of centre. Simultaneously, there was a decrease in the shares for sectors with a great number of production units.

In the first study mentioned above the grouping of centres was taken as given and in the second, also the grouping of sectors was given. A more satisfactory procedure would be to use some kind of method which, by itself, produces the grouping. We thereby encounter problems concerning identification of industrial complexes. Two definitions of such complexes exist. One is based on the idea that sectors cooperate functionally, while the other sees an industrial complex as a set of sectors situated in the same location (Roepke et al., 1974). According to the first definition, sectors are clustered according to flows of goods, that is, input-output coefficients are used as data. The most common statistical method is factor analysis (Andersson, 1973), (Roepke et al., 1974).[2]

It is not functional dependencies, but the extent to which sectors are concentrated to the same types of centre that is of interest for this study; that is, the second definition of complex. Britton (1973) discusses the possibilities of using component analysis to group centres according to their composition. The purpose is, on the one hand, to identify centres with similar composition and, on the other, sectors that are concentrated to the same type of centre. Britton points out that component analysis, in certain conditions, makes these two groupings simultaneously. By pairwise comparison of component values and factor loadings it is then possible to identify the sector blocks within the respective type of centre. The study also calls attention to the fact that component analysis is unsuitable when data are correlated with more than one component, which is the case when the system of centres is hierarchical. Britton therefore only uses the method to reduce the original data material. The final grouping is made by factor analysis.

Britton does not rank centres. This is, however, done by Berry and Barnum (1962). By component analysis, they identify three levels of the system of centres in the United States (Villages, Towns, Cities), and three sector groups. In studying the continuity of sectors, that is, when sector groups and types of centre are brought together, the authors make comparisons in pairs of factor loadings and component values. As we pointed out earlier, this approach is unsuitable when the system of centres has structural elements that are common to several types of centre.

In this study, component analysis is used to group sectors according to similarity of location and Swedish municipal blocks by similarity in sector composition. In studying whether the sectors are continuous, they are brought together with types of centre. However, factors loading and component values are not compared. Instead sector groups and types of centre are combined on the basis of a table.

3.2. AN EMPIRICAL INVESTIGATION FOR SWEDEN

3.2.1. Approach and results
Data concerning the number of plants distributed among municipal blocks have been taken from the Swedish Industrial Statistics (1971) and are restricted to the manufacturing industry. Altogether the material covers 141 sectors.[3]

One weakness of the investigation is that it does not include the service sectors. This is entirely due to the fact that data for these activities were not available. However, studies from other countries show that the service sectors are, in general, continuous (Berry and Barnum, 1962). No corresponding studies exist for the manufacturing industry. To a certain extent, the present study may fill up this gap.

Since a great part of the economy is not included, our conclusions concerning ranking of centres and sectors are of course uncertain. But since the influence of the manufacturing industry is probably considerably greater than this industry's share of the national income, the study should still demonstrate certain fundamental traits of the Swedish system of centres.

Since the location of a manufacturing plant is usually assumed to be less sensitive to distance than the location of service sectors, it is sometimes pointed out that manufacturing can be located in small centres and at the same time serve the whole country. It is, therefore, justifiable to ask whether there exists an obvious regularity in the locational behaviour of manufacturing. Some authors have maintained that the hierarchy models can only explain the location of the service sectors (Richardson, 1973a, p. 73). Tinbergen's model, however, also aims at explaining the location of the manufacturing industry. Our particular interest in this model therefore provides further reasons for giving special attention to manufacturing.

The differences between factors determining the location of manufacturing and services have probably been reduced with time. Economies of scale are usually assumed to characterize manufacturing, while transportation costs are assumed important to the production of services. The present tendency towards concentration and increasing travel distances for the service sectors show, however, that economies of scale are important also to these activities.

The importance of economies of scale to the production of services is evident when comparing a small region to a metropolitan region. The Lycksele region and the Stockholm region have been compared by studying the professional registers of the telephone directory (Andersson et al., 1970, p. 7:31). A good 80 per cent of the service available in Stockholm is out of reach in Lycksele, without long journeys. Like manufacturing, the production of services is all the more oriented towards considerably larger markets than that of a single region. This makes it possible to consider manufacturing as an example which allows for generalizations to other sectors of the Swedish system of centres.

The municipal blocks, according to the division valid 1971, constitute as a rule the geographical units of the investigation. Since the metropolitan areas (Stockholm, Gothenburg and Malmö) must be considered as relatively well-integrated units it seemed unsuitable to divide these into individual municipal blocks. Each of the metropolitan areas is therefore considered as one centre. Together with the remaining municipal blocks there is a total of 237 centres. Appendix 1 includes a list of the municipal blocks belonging to the metropolitan areas, as well as a ranking of all centres according to population. This ranking is based on a special study of the population in 1970 within an area of radius 5 km from the municipal block centre, carried out by ERU.[4] Because of the restricted capacity of the data program used, it has not been possible to include all municipal blocks. Thus the results refer to the 190 biggest blocks.

Component analysis is most reliable when all variables are measured in the same unit. If the scale is changed for one, or several of the variables, the covariance matrix and the components also change (Lawley and Maxwell, 1963, p. 47). Should the variable measure characteristics that are not directly comparable, the problem is usually solved by standardizing all variables. In the present case it is a qualitative characteristic that is of interest, namely, whether the variables posses a characteristic or not. It is not the number of plants for a sector in a municipal block that is decisive in this case, but the existence or absence of a sector. The variables have only two values: one if a sector is represented in a centre, and zero in other cases. With this representation there is no lack of clarity concerning the scale. Furthermore the 0, 1 – representation has a characteristic that is valuable when interpreting the component analysis. The total variation is namely equal to the number of ones. Explained variance, corresponding to each set of components, is thereby made meaningful by denoting the share of the total number of plants explained by this set.

The method is illustrated by an example presented in tables 3.1 and 3.2.

Table 3.1. Unstructured data.

Municipal blocks	Sectors				
	I	II	III	IV	V
A	1	1	1	1	1
B	0	0	0	0	1
C	1	0	1	0	1
D	1	1	1	1	1
E	0	0	0	0	1

Table 3.2. Structured data.

Municipal Blocks	Sectors				
	V	I	III	II	IV
A	1	1	1	1	1
D	1	1	1	1	1
C	1	1	1	0	0
B	1	0	0	0	0
E	1	0	0	0	0

The ones denote in which of the five municipal blocks, A–E, the sectors I–V have at least one plant. Zero denotes the absence of plants. Table 3.1 presents unstructured data. A limited data base often makes it possible to judge at once whether there is a pattern or not; for example, whether sectors are continuous. Otherwise some method must be used to restructure the material in order to facilitate the interpretation. Component analysis makes it possible to transform the data of table 3.1 to make the pattern of table 3.2 stand out clearly. It is then possible to discern three types of centre and three sector groups, that is:

	$h = 1$	$h = 2$	$h = 3$
Sector	V	I, III	II, IV
Centre	B, E	C	A, D

The investigation for the Swedish system of centres leads to a situation where the first three components account for half of the total number of plants.[5] These are dimensions with a considerable influence on the system of centres, and for this reason they are given special attention. The other components show relatively small variances. With ten components, only 10 per cent more of the variation has been explained, and it is only after 70 components that 95 per cent of the plants have been accounted for. That the explained variation increases so slowly indicates the importance of sector-specific and stochastic locational behaviour.

No clear rules exist to determine the number of components to be included. An evaluation must be done in every single case. The value of the results must therefore be seen against the number of components included. If the number of components increases, more specific groups will show up. The question is, therefore, whether it is possible to find a small number of components indicating different levels in the system of centres. It was found suitable to limit the study mainly to the first three components. With low correlations the components 4 to 10 were studied as well.

The municipal blocks are clustered according to component values and allotted to the component with the highest absolute value for this block (see appendix 2). The study indicates the existence of three types of centre in the Swedish system of centres. The highest-ranking type contains the ten largest centres (component 2), the middle-ranking type includes the next fifty centres (components 1 and 3) and the third one, finally, consists of all centres smaller than the sixty largest centres. Centres of the lowest-ranking type are here distributed among all ten components included, and for this reason this type is less homogenous than the other two types. The reason for combining these centres into one type is that individual clusters cannot be ranked according to size of centres included. The middle-ranking type also includes centres that have been brought together by different components. As it appears from appendices 1 and 2, the most important towns of the northern part of Sweden belong to the type determined by component three, while the other type includes only one town in the north. This difference in the middle-ranking type between the north of Sweden and the rest of the country will be further dealt with later.

The picture obtained when studying ten components is summarized in figure 3.1.

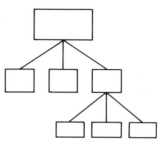

Figure 3.1.

The first level represents the starting-point where all municipalities belong to the same group. On the next level (corresponding to the first three components) the hierarchy evidences itself. Three types of centre can be distinguished; one including the ten largest centres. The next fifty municipal blocks follow as a second type. The third type includes all remaining centres. On the third level, representing components 4 to 10, mainly small centres are clustered. These cannot be ranked among themselves.

In urban economics, a group of metropolitan areas is usually distinguished. These areas are taken to possess special characteristics because of their size. Such a group has not been identified in this study. One reason for this is probably that the service sectors have not been included.

The clustering of sectors has been made with respect of factor loadings and the result is presented in appendix 3. Four groups, (a–d), stand out in particular. All these are grouped on one of the first three components and together correspond to ca. 75 per cent of the sectors included in the study.

As was stressed in the preceding section and is also shown in the supplement, component analysis implies intercorrelation between clusters if the system of centres is in accord with Tinbergen's hypothesis. This makes the use of factor loadings and component values unsuitable in bringing together sector groups and corresponding types of centre. Instead of using an additional numerical procedure, sector groups and types of centre are brought together as in table 3.3.

The purpose of the investigation is to find out at which levels in the system of centres the sector groups occur. Another interesting characteristic is whether or not the sectors are continuous. By dividing the actual number of ones by the product of the number of sectors and the number of municipal blocks for each centre-sector combination, a measure is obtained that reveals the occurrence of these sectors within the type of centre. The calculations are presented in table 3.3.

Table 3.3. The occurrence of sector clusters on different levels in the hierarchy of centres.[6]

a. The four most important clusters.

Type of centre	Second cluster a	b	c	d
1–10	0,83	0,64	0,63	0,62
11–60[7]	0,71	0,39	0,31	0,17
11–60[8]	0,56	0,09	0,37	0,08
61–190	0,41	0,21	0,11	0,04

b. Clusters with a small number of sectors in each cluster.

Type of centre	e	f	g	h	i	Sector cluster j	k	l	m	n	o	p	q
1–10	0,67	0,17	0,50	0,66	0,66	0,42	0,63	0,72	0,67	0,71	0,50	0,83	0,38
11–60[7]	0,67	0,15	0,55	0,10	0,20	0,29	0,30	0,35	0,25	0,13	0,16	0,35	0,24
11–60[8]	0,61	0,26	0,11	0,05	0,11	0,16	0,20	0,25	0,14	0,05	0,09	0,42	0,07
61–190	0,54	0,15	0,16	0,08	0,04	0,15	0,13	0,14	0,12	0,08	0,07	0,16	0,09

The sector clusters e–q in table 3.3b are small, and therefore less important to the explanation of the three types of centre. Table 3.3a, however, summarizes the locations of the four big groups. A sample of sectors taken from these groups is presented in table 3.4. A complete presentation is to be found in appendix 3.

Out of a total of 141 sectors, 105 belong to the four biggest groups. The distribution of the sectors among the group is:

Group	Number of sectors
a	15
b	15
c	21
d	54

Group a is present on all three levels of centres. Two groups, b and c, have low values for the level with the smallest centres, but are represented on the other two levels. Group d only reaches a sufficiently high value on the highest level, that is, in the largest cities, but is otherwise poorly represented.

Table 3.4. An arbitrary choice of sectors within the groups (a–d).

Group a

Manufacture of dairy products
Manufacture of bakery products
Printing and newspaper publishing
Manufacture of concrete and concrete products
Manufacture of structural metal products

Group b

Knitting mills
Manufacture of wearing apparel – outerwear
Manufacture of unholstered furniture
Manufacture of cutlery, hand tools and general hardware

Group c

Slaughtering
Preparing and preserving meat
Malt liquors and malt
Manufacture of pulp
Manufacture of radio, television and communication equipment and apparatus

---

Group d

Coffee roasting
Manufacture of made-up textile goods except wearing apparel
Manufacture of containers and boxes of paper and paperboard
Bookbinding
Manufacture of drugs and medecines

3.2.2. Some comments on the result

We will try to evaluate the results despite weaknesses in their foundation. Here further empirical research is required. Component analysis can only hint at the realism of the different models presented in the previous chapter. Table 3.3. supports the assumption that the occurrence of continuous sectors is frequent in the Swedish system of centres.[9] In other words, the explanatory value seems to be greater in the models of Christaller and Tinbergen than in Lösch's model. On the other hand, the division of the type of centre 11–60 between towns in the north of Sweden and towns in the rest of the country shows that the composition of centres is more irregular than the one proposed by Tinbergen and Christaller.

The centre composition and the relations between ordered types of centre prescribed by Tinbergen only hold if certain conditions are fulfilled. One such condition is that the production based on natural resources, for example, agriculture and forestry, is evenly distributed in space. A study of Bos was presented earlier where input-output coefficients were introduced in Tinbergen's model. Bos states that Tinbergen's hypothesis must then be revised, but not in any decisive way. Tinbergen's hypothesis has probably also to be adjusted in the case of changes in assumptions on the location of natural resources.

Table 3.3a shows that towns in the north of Sweden belonging to the intermediate type of centre lack the sector group b. This sector group is, however, represented in other centres within the type. Group b. contains sectors which to a great extent had their locational pattern determined during the industrialization phase; the textile industry, for example. The industrialization process was concentrated to the south and middle of Sweden, where the increase in the agricultural population offered the labour surplus necessary to manufacturing. In the northern part of Sweden the supply of labour was never as great, since forestry provided a supplementary income which allowed the population to stay within agriculture. The deviation noted in relation to Tinbergen's model may therefore be due to the fact that the actual distribution of Swedish agriculture and forestry differs from the distribution that forms the basis of the model.

The result indicates that models based on continuous sectors (Christaller and Tinbergen) better reflect the Swedish system of centres than Lösch's model. A hierarchy with three types of centre has been identified. The hierarchy of centres is principally based on four sector groups. From table 3.3a, it follows that the sectors are continuous, that is, they lack in centres below a certain rank and exist in all centres above this rank.[10] As a rule, the sectors in table 3.3b are continuous too.

Comparing Tinbergen's model with Christaller's, it is striking how well our results agree with Tinbergen's hypothesis of a ratio of one to four between the number of centres of one rank and the centres of the next lowest rank (Mennes et al., 1969, p. 224). Christaller's corresponding ratio is one to three. If we start from the number of ten for the type with the largest centres, a Tinbergen system implies 10.40.160. with 210 centres altogether. If, in the present study, we also consider the smallest municipal blocks, those excluded because of calculation difficulties, we obtain a distribution of the 237 municipal blocks corresponding to 10.50.177.

Tinbergen (Mennes et al., 1969, p. 211) assumes a relationship between the number of plants in a sector and the location of the sector. It is assumed that a sector hierarchy corresponds to the hierarchy of centres in such a way that sectors with a small number of plants only exist in the largest centres; that it is possible to group the sectors so that, when moving down the hierarchy of centres, for each level there is a corresponding group of sectors with a gradually increasing number of plants. In our study this would mean that the number of plants for the sectors in group a. should, on average, be greater than the number of plants for the other groups in table 3.3a. The average in b and c should be lower than in a, while sector group d. should have the lowest average.

From appendix 3 it follows that the number of plants for sectors in a. is usually bigger than for other groups. In some cases the number is small, but the factor loadings are then also low. The other groups also correspond in the main to Tinbergen's assumption. Just as for a, some cases occur with too small a number of plants and low factor loadings. It should be noted that sector groups corresponding to the two highest-ranking types of centre in some cases have more plants than is motivated by their position in the hierarchy. This is particularly true for certain divisions of the textile industry, but other cases also occur.[11]

As for generalizations to other countries, Berry and Barnum (1962), have obtained results similar to those of the present study, though with data from the United States. Since there are no statistics on deliveries, relations between different types of centre have not been studied. The numerical examples in chapter 4, where, among other things, deliveries within the system are determined, are intended to compensate for this weakness in the empirical data.

Supplement

Component analysis – presentation and use

Component analysis implies the transformation of a set of observed (manifest) variables $(x_1, x_2, \ldots x_p)$ to a new set (latent) $(y_1, y_2, \ldots y_p)$, where the new variables are uncorrelated. In some contexts, this is called orthogonal transformation. When the original variables have a certain total variance it is characteristic of the method that y_1 extracts the maximum possible variance. The second variable (component) extracts the maximum possible variance from the normal hyperplane to component 1 and so on, until all variance is explained, requiring a maximum of p components.[12] Thus component analysis is not derived from any economic model.

This presentation of component analysis is based on Hadley (1969), Harman (1960), King (1969) and Lawley and Maxwell (1963). Figure 3.2 illustrates the procedure in a simple way, with x_1 and x_2 as two correlated variables. The assumption of correlation and normal distribution leads to an elliptic form of the two-dimensional distribution, with the axis of the ellipse rotated according to an angle of θ in relation to the co-ordinate system.

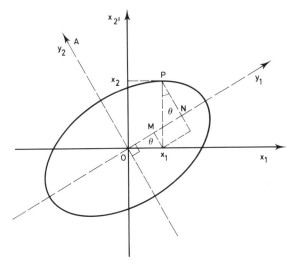

Figure 3.2.

Component analysis is a method of finding the matrix that transforms the correlated variables x_1 and x_2 to the uncorrelated y_1 and y_2. It is thus possible to express the y-co-ordinates for P in x_1 and x_2 as

$$y_1 = OM + MN = x_1 \cos \theta + x_2 \sin \theta$$

y_2 is determined in a similar way

$$y_2 = -x_1 \sin \theta + x_2 \cos \theta$$

With the help of a matrix, the transformation can be written:[13]

$$y^T = Ux^T$$

where

$$y^T = \begin{bmatrix} y_1 \\ y_2 \end{bmatrix}; \ x^T = \begin{bmatrix} x_1 \\ x_2 \end{bmatrix} \text{ and}$$

$$U = \begin{bmatrix} \cos \theta \ \sin \theta \\ -\sin \theta \ \cos \theta \end{bmatrix}$$

This may be generalized to p variables with observations for n cases. We then set out from a matrix of observations, X, where the columns represent variables and the rows cases. Thus, X is an n by p matrix. The basic model of the component analysis can now be written:

$$X = YQ \tag{3.1}$$

Y, the matrix of component values, is also an n by p matrix, where the columns represent components. Q is a pth order quadratic matrix.

Q is orthogonal, that is

$$Q^T Q = I$$

where I is an identity matrix. Since the product of a matrix and its inverse is always equal to the identity matrix, the inverse and the transpose of an orthogonal matrix must be identical, that is

$$Q^T = Q^{-1}$$

As was mentioned earlier, the problem focuses on variation. The variances of the uncorrelated variables y_1, y_2 ... are therefore defined. Thereby it is not assumed that the x-variables are standardized but however, that their mean values are zero.[14]
The variances are:

$$\Lambda = Y^T Y = QX^T XQ^T = QAQ^T \tag{3.2}$$

A is the covariance matrix of the x-variables, while Λ has the variance of the y-variables as diagonal elements and contains otherwise only zeros. These qualities of the matrix Λ are due to the fact that the components are uncorrelated, which also requires that Q is an orthogonal matrix. This quality of Q will be further treated later.

(3.2) is a characteristic value problem. The eigenvalues of the matrix A are in the diagonal of Λ, that is, they correspond to the variances of the uncorrelated variables. One characteristic of Λ is that the first eigenvalue (the variance of y_1) is the greatest, the second is the next greatest, and so on. This agrees with that said earlier about the first component extracting maximum variance from the data matrix. The second component thereafter extracts the maximum possible variance and so on, until all variation is explained.

Consequently, the sum of all eigenvalues should be equal to the sum of the diagonal elements in A.

A covariance matrix is always symmetric, allowing us to use some known algebraic theorems. The first of these theorems states that eigenvalues are always real when A is symmetric. This symmetry also permits us to check the orthogonality of Q, the matrix of eigenvectors. Another theorem namely states that when A is symmetric, the matrix of eigenvectors is orthogonal (Hadley, 1969, p. 240).

Component analysis can also be discussed as a problem of optimization (johnston, 1972, p. 322), that is, the method can have the same mathematical form as our economic models in chapters 4 and 5. Then the first component is determined by the following programming problem:

$$\max \lambda = \lambda_1 = y_1 y_1^T = q_1 A q_1^T$$

q_1 is chosen to maximize the variance λ. In order to prevent λ_1 from extending beyond all bounds, a constraint is introduced, stating that q_1 is to be a normalized vector, that is

$$q_1 q_1^T = 1$$

The Lagrangean of the programming problem is

$$L = q_1 A q_1^T - \lambda_1'(q_1 q_1^T - 1)$$

where λ_1' is a Lagrange multiplier.

$$\frac{\delta L}{\delta q_1^T} = 2A q_1^T - 2\lambda_1' q_1^T$$

$$\frac{\delta L}{\delta q_1^T} = 0$$

for maximum, that is

$$A q_1^T = \lambda_1' \, q_1^T$$

The expression is a characteristic value problem with the eigenvalue λ_1' and the eigenvector q_1^T. $A q_1^T = \lambda_1' q_1^T$ is inserted into the maximand:

$$\lambda_1 = \lambda_1' \, q_1 q_1^T = \lambda_1'$$

The optimization problem thus consists of selecting the greatest eigenvalue of A and then determining the corresponding eigenvector. A is a symmetric, positive definite matrix. The eigenvalue is therefore real.

Thereafter Johnston determines the second component:

$$\max \lambda = \lambda_2 = y_2 y_2^T = q_2 A q_2^T$$

subject to

$$q_2 q_2^T = 1$$

$$q_1 q_2^T = 0$$

The second condition states that the components should be uncorrelated.

The Lagrangean is:

$$L = q_2 A q_2^T - \lambda_2'(q_2 q_2^T - 1) - \mu(q_1 q_2^T)$$

where λ_2' and μ are two Lagrange multipliers.

$$\frac{\delta L}{\delta q_2^T} = 2 A q_2^T - 2\lambda_2' q_2^T - \mu q_1^T$$

The derivative is pre-multiplied by q_1:

$$2 q_1 A q_2^T - \mu = 0$$

The following is known from the determination of the first component:

$$A q_1^T = \lambda_1' q_1^T$$

After pre-multiplying by q_2 the following is obtained:

$$q_2 A q_1^T = \lambda_1' q_2 q_1^T = 0$$

that is, $\mu = 0$ and

$$A q_2^T = \lambda_2' q_2^T$$

The expression found is inserted into the maximand:

$$\lambda_2 = \lambda_2' q_2 q_2^T = \lambda_2'$$

The maximization procedure is repeated until all variance is extracted. Finally, Johnston's presentation is summarized in the following programming model:

$$\max q_i A q_i^T$$

subject to

$$q_i q_i^T = 1$$

$$q_h q_i^T = 0 \qquad h = 1 \dots i - 1$$

for all i, where $1 \leqq i \leqq p$. p is the number of manifest variables.

How can component analysis be used? One way is to employ the method to restructure variables to an equal number of uncorrelated components, or fewer. The first of these components has the greatest variance, the second has the next greatest variance etc. This, the most direct application of component analysis, is sometimes used in numerical contexts when a set of uncorrelated variables is desired (Mårdberg, 1969, p. 51).

If only some of the components are used – reduced component analysis – the method brings out new dimensions, that is, composite variables which are not directly observable from manifest variables. The components then represent dimensions that are supposed to describe structural characteristics. It is then necessary to indicate an acceptable proportion between explained and original variance. Here, only 'good' thumb-rules exist. It appears, however, that a small number of components generally explain an important part of the variation in data. In all circumstances one can be assured that it is impossible to find another set of an equal number of components, explaining a greater part of the variance of the x-variables (Mårdberg, 1969, p. 52).

In reduced component analysis the matrix of eigenvectors Q is examined. The contexts are best understood if we begin by considering the matrix U, where the rows are eigenvectors. The elements of the eigenvectors denote the correlation between x-variables and components in the following manner. The first element of the first eigenvector ($\cos \phi$) is the correlation between x_1 and y_1, the second element ($\sin \phi$) is the correlation between x_2 and y_1. In a similar way, the second eigenvector expresses the correlations with the second component (y_2). To link up to Q, the coefficients in the first row express the correlation of the different x-variables with the first component. If the coefficients are denoted q_{ij}, where i refers to row and j to column, q_{ij} indicates the correlation between the x-variable j and component i. q_{ij} is called factor loading.

In reduced component analysis factor loadings can be used to give the components a tentative interpretation. Characteristics of observed variables with high factor loadings on a component are then examined. The component is thereby seen as a manifestation of something that these variables have in common. Assume that the rows in X account for the consumption behaviour of different individuals, so that the columns correspond to consumer goods. Two components are assumed sufficient to extract all variance from X. The first one is constituted by consumption of public goods, while only private utilities are correlated with component two. By guessing, the consumption of public goods is related to whether a person lives in a rural or urban area, in the centre of a town or in a suburb. The conclusion should preferably be that the first component is a variable with an impact on consumption which is related to where people live. The second component probably reflects differences in income.

In large-scale investigations, the observed variables are often so numerous that the material is difficult to interpret. Since it is the variation that is interesting, a suitable method should structure data in order to bring out dimensions with large variance. When investigating characteristics of consumption, for example, it is suitable to begin with consumption where differences between individuals are great. Since component analysis successively brings out components which in each step have maximum variance, the method is in this respect particularly suitable.

Another problem in reduced component analysis is to restructure the data to a summarizing form, so-called cluster analysis. It is in this way the method is used in the present study. This method of application is underpinned, however, by the assumption that the clusters can be interpreted in a meaningful way. The problem in cluster analysis is that of combining variables or cases to homogenous groups, given measurements of certain characteristics. A seemingly reasonable principle is to group variables with regard to common variance, that is, according to the part of the variance of a variable that is explained by covariance with one or several other variables. In component analysis it holds that variables with high factor loadings on a component are internally correlated and consequently form a group.

As was indicated in 3.1, component analysis sometimes has been used in studies of how groups of cases are built up from found variable dimensions (Berry and Barnum, 1962). In studies of systems of centres, component analysis has, for example, been used to identify the sector groups that compose the types of centre. Centres have been grouped in relation to component values, and sectors on the basis of factor loadings. In 3.1 it was also established that this procedure is unsuitable when data are correlated with several components. This type of correlation emerged when the sectors in the system of centres are continuous. In spite of this, Berry and Barnum (1962) combine sector groups and types of centre by pairwise comparisons of factor loadings and component scores. This problem will be discussed somewhat more extensively.

In figure 3.3, two different structures of variables and cases are represented. Let us link up to our empirical problem and assume that the variables correspond to economic sectors and that the cases are geographical centres. Assume also that the variables can only have the values zero or one. Zero implies that the sector is absent in a centre, and one that it is present. If the lined surfaces represent such combinations of centres and sectors which give ones, then 3.3a represents a structure of the system of centres according to the systems of Christaller and Tinbergen. Vertical rectangles represent sector ranks and horizontal rectangles types of centre. The size of the centres of a group increases thereby when the distance of the group from the horizontal axis increases. When a sector has occurred in a type of centre, it is also present in all types with larger centres. In 3.3b, however, the sectors are specific for the centres; that is, a sector only exists within one type of centre. Our empirical problem is to identify the groups of cases and variables which belong to the lined fields in figure 3.3.

The relations between variables and cases are sought by pairwise comparisons of components calculated on the basis of X and X^T, respectively. Those which in X constitute variables become cases in X^T, and vice versa. The proof is based on a theorem of Yasida (1960), p. 120). Our starting-point is the basic model (3.1) and its counterpart for X^T, which is

$$X^T = DB \qquad (3.3)$$

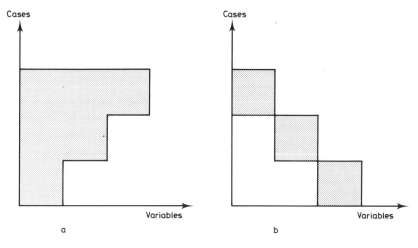

Figure 3.3

In (3.3), B is an nth order quadratic transformation matrix, and D is a p by n component score matrix with the components in the columns. B is assumed to be orthogonal, and thus (3.3) can be written as $D = (XB)^T$. The following expression for the variance of components is obtained:

$$D^T D = BXX^T B^T = BRB^T$$

R is an nth order covariance matrix. Since R is symmetric we can check that B actually is orthogonal (Hadley, 1969, p. 240).

The eigenvalue equation corresponding to A for the eigenvalue λ_i can be written

$$A q_i^T = \lambda_i q_i^T$$

where q_i is an arbitrarily chosen row vector in Q. The following equation is introduced

$$z_i^T = 1/\sqrt{\lambda_i}\ X\ q_i^T \tag{3.4}$$

where it is assumed that $\lambda_i > 0$

First, it is shown that z_i^T is a normalized vector:

$$z_i z_i^T = 1/\lambda_i q_i\ X^T\ X\ q_i^T = 1/\lambda_i\ q_i\ A\ q_i^T = \frac{\lambda_i}{\lambda_i} q_i\ q_i^T = 1$$

It will now be demonstrated that z_i is a normalized eigenvector to R:

$$Rz_i^T = XX^T 1/\sqrt{\lambda_i}\, X\, q_i^T = 1/\sqrt{\lambda_i}\, X\, A\, q_i^T = 1/\sqrt{\lambda_i}\, X\, \lambda_i\, q_i^T$$
$$= \lambda_i z_i^T$$

The procedure is carried out for all eigenvectors in Q. It is then found that the corresponding z_i is an eigenvector in B. Furthermore, the eigenvalues are the same for the pairs of components.

We go on to show how Yasida's theorem can be used within the component analysis. When the diagonal elements in A and R, respectively, are summed up, the sums are equal, that is, total variance in X and X^T is equal. If p is less than n, this implies that the eigenvalues of R, corresponding to the difference between n and p, have to be zero. Since the total variation in R is thus extracted after p eigenvectors, the remaining vectors are of no interest. We therefore introduce a new matrix, $\overline{B}^{\,T}$, which is an n by p matrix. The matrix corresponds to B when eigenvectors with the eigenvalue zero have been removed.

If we make use of the relation between eigenvectors for pairs of components, (3.4), (3.1) can be written as:

$$X = \overline{B}^{\,T} \Lambda^{1/2} Q \qquad\qquad (3.1')$$

Y, the component value matrix in (3.1), is evidently $Y = \overline{B}^{\,T} \Lambda^{1/2}$ or $\overline{B}^T = Y \Lambda^{-1/2}$. Since the eigenvector matrix B can be determined by standardizing Y, that is, by post-multiplying by Λ^{-2}, the basic model (3.1) is sufficient to group both variables and cases. Some authors sometimes use the standardized form of Y to indicate the components (Lawley and Maxwell, 1963). If the standardized form is used, (3.1') shows that component analysis can be used in investigations of how clusters of cases are built up by variables. This is obtained by pairwise comparisons of factor loadings and components scores.

The method can be illustrated by an example from Mårdberg (1969). Mårdberg starts out from dimensions and other technical data on cars. The cars serve as cases and their characteristics as variables. First, a covariance matrix for the 13 variables was calculated. This was used to determine the standardized component score matrix, $\overline{B}^{\,T}$, and factor loadings, Q. The first component was interpreted as a dimension of size. This component had the highest factor loadings for variables such as weight, length, breadth, volume of the fuel tank, number of cylinders etc. Cars with high component scores were generally big. Small cars had the lowest scores. The second component had high factor loadings for the number of doors, seats, and the height of the car. The highest component scores were obtained by cars with relatively numerous doors and seats, and high heights. Sport cars had the lowest scores. Mårdberg discusses two more components that are excluded here.

In consequence, an observation in X, for example x_{ij}, can be regarded as a weighting of the correlation of the variable j and the case i with the components, or

$$x_{ij} = \sum_{z=1}^{P} \lambda_z^{1/2} \, b_{iz} \, q_{zj} \qquad\qquad (3.5)$$

where b_{iz} denotes the coefficient of correlation for case i with respect to component z. In a similar way, q_{zj} indicates the correlation between the variable j and component z. In order to keep x_{ij} differentiated from zero, the case i and the variable j must be correlated with the same components.

If a sector exists in a centre in figure 3.3 (3.5) shows that the sector and the centre should be correlated with the same components. For an arbitrary centre-sector combination in figure 3.3b, it holds that the pair is only correlated with one component. Here, sectors and centres within a group pair are thus uncorrelated with components for other groups. In 3.2a the situation is different. By using (3.5) we find that a sector group is correlated with components for centres from separate types of centre. A similar correlation is to be found between sector groups.

Component analysis is best suited to solving problems of grouping like the one in figure 3.3b. By pairwise comparison of factor loadings and component scores, ones are obtained within the lined areas and zeros in other positions. In figure 3.3a, however, there is intercorrelation between groups. Problems may arise, therefore, of identifying sector groups and types of centre. This is why it is unsuitable to examine relations between centres and sectors by pairwise comparisons of component scores and factor loadings. In the empirical study in 3.2 it was assumed that if sectors are grouped on that component for which the sector has its highest factor loading, a good approximation of actual sector groups is obtained. A similar grouping of centres with respect to standardized component scores was assumed to reflect geographical levels of the system of centres. On the other hand, it was not considered suitable to examine the existence of continuous sectors by pairwise comparisons of factor loadings and component scores. This second step was therefore carried out in a table.

NOTES

1. Those unfamiliar with the concepts used in component analysis should begin by reading the supplement to chapter 3.
2. A presentation of factor analysis is to be found, for example, in Harman (1960).
3. The Swedish standard for classification is identical to ISIC up to and including the four digit level and has one more subclassification.
4. The Expert Group on Regional Studies at the Swedish Labour Market Ministry.
5. Ca. 50 per cent of the total data variation.
6. The division into three levels is based on the result from the clustering of municipal blocks. Then small municipal blocks (with low component values) grouped on components 1 and 3, have been transferred to group $61 \leqq h \leqq 190$.
7. Subdivision corresponding to component 1, that is, the cluster where towns in the south of Sweden are over-represented.
8. Subdivision corresponding to component 3, that is, the cluster were towns in the north of Sweden are over-represented.
9. A sector h' is continuous if it exists in all centres of rank $\geqq h'$. See also the definition of a continuous sector in section 2.2.2.
10. Note that the study only refers to the manufacturing industry.
11. The variation in the number of plants between sectors within a group may also be due to the classification of sectors. If, for example, the textile industry also contains boutiques, the number of plants is naturally greater than for a sector with the same pattern of location, but where retailing is included in another group than the sector itself.
12. The standardized form is referred to as components by some authors (Lawley and Maxwell, 1963). Here it is assumed that the y-variables represent the components.
13. In the following the transpose denotes a column vector.
14. The assumption is necessary if $X^T X$ is to be a covariance matrix.

4. An attempt to extend the problem of Tinbergen and Bos – capacities of plants given

4.1. PRESENTATION OF THE PROBLEM

The subject of this chapter is the formulation of a programming model. The model includes input-output coefficients. Indivisibilities and transportation costs are also taken into consideration. Capacities of plants are given. Consequently, the importance of location choices to the size of plants has not been dealt with. An alternative formulation is put forward in chapter 5, where capacities and spatial dispersion are determined simultaneously. Section 4.3 deals with the model itself, and is followed by a section with some numerical examples testing Tinbergen's hypothesis. In the first two the optimal structure of the system of centres is compared for different values on the coefficient relating final demand for agriculture to total income. The purpose of the third example is to show the nature of optimum with different spatial distributions of agriculture and other natural resources.

One of our hypotheses is that individual decision-making, based on price information, leads to a situation where the biggest centres contain more activities than is optimal with regard to transportation costs. An agglomeration effect of this kind has been discussed earlier, for instance, by Hotelling (1929) and Serck-Hanssen (1970). Hotelling sets out from the particular case of duopoly, where each seller adjusts his price and location so that, with existing price and location of the competitor, his own profit will be maximized. If they both locate along an evenly populated line, only one steady-state equilibrium is existent, that is, when they both settle down next to each other in the centre of the line. This equilibrium is unacceptable, as there are other locations with lower transportation costs.

The location of department stores seems to be the classic ex-

ample of the phenomenon discussed by Hotelling. Department
stores usually locate next to each other for instance within city
centres.[1]

Serck-Hanssen's approach (1970, p. 36) is based on other assumptions. He sets out from a situation where agriculture ($h = 0$) is evenly
distributed along a line. In addition, H factories separately produce
one of the commodities $h = 1, 2 \ldots H$. Each factory delivers a unit
of goods to each one of the other $H - 1$ factories. The cost of transporting one unit of goods one distance unit is the same, irrespective
of the factory from which the good comes. This cost is equal to t.
Each factory exchanges goods with agriculture, at a cost corresponding to t_0 per unit of distance transported.

To begin with, all factories – and these are more than two – are
located together in an agglomeration in the centre of the line. It is
assumed that, when a factory moves out of the agglomeration, the
distance to agriculture diminishes by one distance unit. Simultaneously, the distance from the centre increases to the same extent.
This implies that a simple move out from the centre reduces transportation costs for exchanges of goods with agriculture by t_0. Simultaneously, transportation costs to and from factories in the
agglomeration increase by $2t(H - 1)$.

The condition for a profitable move out is:

(4.1) $t_0 > 2t(H - 1)$

If, on the other hand, K factories move ($K \leqq H/2$), transportation
costs for exchanges with agriculture diminish by Kt_0, while transportation costs to and from the agglomeration increase by $2Kt$
$(H - K)$.

The condition for a profitable division of the centre into two
halves is:

(4.2) $t_0 > tH$

For values of H where (4.2) holds but not (4.1), the market mechanism emits incorrect signals. The result is that centres which, in fact,
should be split up, remain unchanged in size because of individual
decision-making. The situation is illustrated in figure 4.1.

In the figure it is assumed that t is less than half the transporta-

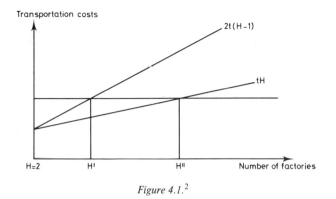

Figure 4.1.[2]

tion costs for exchange with agriculture. If this requirement is not met, that is, if $t \geq \frac{1}{2} t_0$, market signals are always correct. Both $2t (H - 1)$ and tH then exceed t_0 for all $H \geq 2$. Economic evaluation, at both the micro- and macro-level, shows that the centre should not be split up. If t is less than half t_0, there is an interval for the number of factories where market signals are not correct ($H'H''$). (4.2) would inform a planning authority of the desirability of splitting up the centre, while (4.1) shows that a single factory lacks incentives to move. The centre attains a stabilized situation, which is not optimal with regard to transportation costs.[3]

The compatibility of entrepreneurial behaviour with Tinbergen-Bos general location system has been investigated by Paelinck and Nijkamp (1975, p. 136) in a case with two industries producing final and intermediate products. Their conclusion is that certain market structures imply a continuous disequilibrium situation. An equilibrium can only be maintained under special institutional conditions, for instance with the aid of regional intervention.

We will return to the problem of co-ordinating private and public decision-making. The starting-point will be the dual corresponding to the programming model in 4.3. Here, it is the system of centres corresponding to the global optimum that is of importance to public decision-making. If this system is to be maintained when decisions are individual and based on price information, the global optimum must imply that all micro-units lack incentives to relocate. This problem is discussed in 4.5. If it is not possible to interpret the dual variables as prices, the next task will be to investigate the possible nature of an alternative system of implementation. This question is also discussed in 4.5.

In 2.1, conditions for a hierarchy of centres were discussed:

– agricultural production and population are spread over a given area
– the production of non-agricultural industries is characterized by indivisibilities leading to economies of scale
– transports of goods and services give rise to transportation costs

Bos (1965, p. 48) has investigated some simple cases where these conditions are realized. Three types of centre and two non-agricultural sectors are assumed. Only final products are produced. Bos finds that supplementary conditions are necessary to provide an optimal system of centres with the same qualities as in Tinbergen's hypothesis. Bos discusses supplementary conditions using three different transportation cost criteria.

The transportation cost criteria are:

1. Costs depend on type and quantity of goods, but not on distance.
2. The cost of transport between two centres[4] equals the highest cost of the two flows in opposite directions. The cost of a single commodity is calculated as in 1.
3. Costs depend on type, quantity and distance of goods.

For optimum 1 and 2 imply that all production (except agriculture) is concentrated to one or a few centres. For 2, this does not generally hold. When transportation costs for single commodities are zero, no unique solution exists. For 3, it is difficult to make any general statement. However, Bos indicates a certain number of tendencies. One of these is that high transportation costs for sectors of low rank (with many plants) seem to indicate that systems of centres corresponding to Tinbergen's hypothesis are optimal.

According to Bos, Tinbergen's hypothesis does not have to be changed in any degree worth mentioning when input-output coefficients are introduced. The only exception is when single products are directed principally to one or a few sectors. This has been discussed in 2.3. Bos, however, does not base his theory on any programming model and thus does not show if this conclusion is consistent with minimized transportation costs.

4.2. MODELS FOR TESTING WHETHER A CENTRE SHOULD BE SPLIT UP

To the best of our knowlege, sensitivity analyses have, up to now, only concerned assumptions of transportation costs. Bos's analysis of 'link effects' in input-output coefficients is the only exception. An elaboration of the latter is particularly important when analyzing developing countries, where 'a-structurization' is usual and leads to relatively detached, non-integrated units (Amin, 1974, p. 302). The model in 4.3 could possibly be used as a starting-point for a more thorough discussion of such problems.

In our case, other aspects are studied; for example, natural resources, the influence of their use and location on an optimal system of centres. Agriculture then appears as a particular activity. The use of specific natural resources characterizes agriculture, restricting the sector to places where such resources exist.[5] Remaining sectors are assumed to exist only in urban centres (urban sectors). If agriculture dominates, as is one characteristic of developing countries, the system of centres should have many, and small, centres. (However, reality is different. In most cases the modern sector is concentrated to one or two big cities. This distortion depends on the position of colonial dependence of these countries.) If, on the contrary, urban sectors are important in relation to agriculture, the structure of the system of centres is probably more concentrated. The difference can be explained by the relatively larger share of agricultural consumption on the part of the workers and their families in the first case. If input-output coefficients are assumed, there should also be a tendency to concentration when deliveries of intermediate products between urban sectors are numerous in relation to exchange with the agricultural sector.

The problem will be illustrated by some simple models, considering input-output coefficients and based on one agricultural sector (sector 0), and two sectors located in centres (sectors 1 and 2). The highest-ranking sector (sector 2) has only one production unit, and this is located in h''. h'' is superior to a 'regional' centre, h', and agriculture. It is assumed that sector 1 can be ordered in two different ways. This implies, in the first case, that the part of total output of the sector that is destined for agriculture is produced in the 'regional' centre, while the needs of the superior centre are locally balanced within this centre. This is identical with Bos model (cf. 2.3), but instead of two urban sectors, Bos has three. The present formulation entails an extension in the sense that transportation costs, which are lacking in Bos's model, are here included.

The assumption that sector 1 should be locally balanced in h″ is reasonable if the local demand of the superior centre is at least as great as the plant capacity of sector 1. The second possibility of ordering the sector is therefore based on the assumption that demand in h″ falls below this capacity. The total output of the lowest-ranking sector is then assumed to be produced in the 'regional' centre, in such a way that the demand of the superior centre has to be satisfied by importation from h′.

A third alternative for comparison is also set up, involving the absence of a 'regional' centre. The production of sectors 1 and 2 is instead totally concentrated to the superior centre.

The first way of ordering sector 1 is described by a system of equations (model 1). The same notations as in 2.3 are used. The system of centres reflected by model 1 agrees with Tinbergen's hypothesis.

Model 1:

$$\beta_1 x_1^1 = \gamma_{10} x^0 \tag{4.3}$$

$$\beta_1 x_1^2 = \gamma_{12} x_2^2 \tag{4.4}$$

$$\beta_2 x_2^2 = \gamma_{20} x^0 + \gamma_{21} (x_1^1 + x_1^2) \tag{4.5}$$

(4.3) shows that agriculture's need for commodities from the lowest-ranking sector is completely satisfied from h′. The condition also implies that what is left per output-unit, after subtraction of the internal demand of sector 1, is exclusively directed towards agriculture. Sector 1 is thus locally balanced in the superior centre, h″, satisfying only its won requirements and those of the highest-ranking sector (4.4). The latter, sector 2, only exists in h″ (4.5).

The second way of ordering sector 1, that is, without a local sector in the superior centre (model 2), is written:

Model 2:

$$\beta_1 x_1^1 = \gamma_{10} x^0 + \gamma_{12} x_2^2 \tag{4.6}$$

$$\beta_2\, x_2^2 = \gamma_{20}\, x^0 + \gamma_{21}\, x_1^1 \tag{4.7}$$

(4.6) is the condition of balance for the 'regional' centre h' and (4.7) the condition of balance for h''.

Bos's third transportation criterion is used. ϕ_0, ϕ_1 and ϕ_2 constitute the freight rates per distance unit of the sectors 0, 1 and 2. The distance between the 'regional' centre and the superior centre is one unit of distance. Furthermore, it is assumed possible to disregard the distance between h' and agriculture.

Model 1 is discussed first. An amalgamation of the 'regional' centre with the superior centre is then optimal (in the sense of minimized transportation costs) if the following inequality holds:

$$\phi_1\, \gamma_{10}\, x^0 + \phi_0\, \gamma_{01} \frac{\gamma_{10}}{\beta_1} x^0 < \phi_2 \gamma_{21} \frac{\gamma_{10}}{\beta_1} x^0 \tag{4.8}$$

The inequality states that the increased costs for deliveries between sector 1 and agriculture, implied by the alternative of amalgamation, have to be lower than the costs for deliveries from sector 2 to sector 1, that is, when the latter sector is located in the 'regional' centre. The first term to the left of the inequality indicates costs for deliveries from sector 1 to agriculture when the former sector is located in the superior centre. The other terms refer to the amount of goods required by sector 1; the term next to the left of the inequality refers to costs for deliveries from agriculture when sector 1 is located in h''. The term to the right of the inequality indicates deliveries from sector 2, when sector 1 is located in the 'regional' centre. (4.3) has been used in order to express x_1^1 in x^0. Then (4.8) can be rewritten as:

$$\phi_1\, \gamma_{10} + (\phi_0\, \gamma_{01} - \phi_2\, \gamma_{21}) \frac{\gamma_{10}}{\beta_1} < 0$$

If a concentration to one centre is to be advantageous, it is necessary, but not sufficient, that the expression within parenthesis is less than zero, that is:

$$\frac{\gamma_{21}}{\gamma_{01}} > \frac{\phi_0}{\phi_2} \tag{4.9}$$

In model 2 we have to take deliveries from sector 1 in the 'regional' centre to h'' into consideration. (4.6) – (4.7) are then used to express x_1^1 and x_2^2 in x^0:

$$x_1^1 = \frac{\gamma_{10} + \dfrac{\gamma_{12}\,\gamma_{20}}{\beta_2}}{\beta_1 - \dfrac{\gamma_{12}\,\gamma_{21}}{\beta_2}}\, x^0$$

$$x_2^2 = \frac{1}{\beta_2}\left(\gamma_{20} + \gamma_{21}\,\frac{\gamma_{10} + \dfrac{\gamma_{12}\,\gamma_{20}}{\beta_2}}{\beta_1 - \dfrac{\gamma_{12}\,\gamma_{21}}{\beta_2}}\right) x^0$$

As in the preceding model the evaluation is based on an inequality. This means that a concentration is optimal if the costs for deliveries between sector 1 in h'' and agriculture are lower than the costs for the exchnge between sectors 2 and 1 when sector is located in the 'regional' centre. Eliminating x^0 and rearranging the terms, this inequality is:

$$\phi_1\left(\gamma_{10} - \frac{\gamma_{12}\gamma_{20}}{\beta_2}\right) + \left(\phi_0\gamma_{01} - \phi_2\gamma_{21} - \phi_1\frac{\gamma_{12}\gamma_{21}}{\beta_2}\right)\frac{\gamma_{10} + \dfrac{\gamma_{12}\gamma_{20}}{\beta_2}}{\beta_1 - \dfrac{\gamma_{12}\gamma_{21}}{\beta_2}} < 0$$

The next step is to indicate a necessary condition for a concentration of h'' and h' into one centre. Then we use the following condition, namely $x_1^1 \geq 0$, which means that $\beta_1 - \dfrac{\gamma_{12}\gamma_{21}}{\beta_2} \geq 0$ (see the expression of x_1^1 in x^0). Two reasonable assumptions further are made, namely $\gamma_{10} - \dfrac{\gamma_{12}\gamma_{20}}{\beta_2} \geq 0$ and $\phi_1 = \phi_2 = \phi^x$. Then it is enough to use the second parenthesis in the inequality. If the left side of the inequality is to be less than zero, the following must hold:

$$\frac{\gamma_{21}}{\gamma_{01}}\left(1 + \frac{\gamma_{12}}{\beta_2}\right) > \frac{\phi_o}{\phi^x}{}^6 \tag{4.10}$$

Finally, the notations in 2.3 are used to reformulate (4.9) and (4.10) with respect to a_{ij}, α_i and w_i. The necessary conditions for an advantageous concentration are accordingly:

$$\frac{a_{21} + \alpha_2 w_1}{a_{01} + \alpha_0 w_1} > \frac{\phi_0}{\phi_2} \qquad \text{(Modell 1)} \qquad (4.9')$$

$$\frac{a_{21} + \alpha_2 w_1}{a_{01} + \alpha_{02} w_1} \left(1 + \frac{a_{12} + \alpha_1 w_2}{1 - (a_{22} + \alpha_2 w_2)} \right) > \frac{\phi_0}{\phi^x} \qquad \text{(Modell 2)}$$
$$(4.10')$$

The models show that the transportation cost parameters ϕ_0, ϕ_1 and ϕ_2 do not alone determine the form of the optimal system of centres. We find instead that the number of centres depends on the way characteristics of consumption and production structures, and the relations between freight rates, are related to each other. 'Characteristics' refer in this case to input–output coefficients, ratios between value added and output and coefficients relating final demand to income.[7]

$(4.9')$ – $(4.10')$ show that a concentration into one centre is justified on condition that the coefficients relating final demand for urban sectors (sectors 1 and 2) to income are important in relation to that of agriculture. A similar tendency towards concentration is present when there is considerable exchange of intermediate products between sectors 1 and 2, that is, when values a_{12} and a_{21} are high.

Originally we assumed the choice of one or two centres solely to be a question of proportions between urban sectors, considered as a group, and agriculture. $(4.9')$ and $(4.10')$ show that the relationship between parameters of different sectors within the group of urban sectors is also of importance. No matter which model is chosen, a combination into one centre is only profitable if there are specific relations between the parameters of sectors 1 and 2.

If model 1 holds, a reallocation of consumption from sector 1 to the higher-ranking sector 2 may imply that sectors 1 and 2 are to be located together in one centre. In model 2, such a reallocation of consumption does not necessarily imply that the sectors are to be combined into a single centre. In this case, an increase in the value of α_2 is compensated by a decrease in the value of α_1. In model 2, a high value of internal use per unit produced in sector 2 (a high value of $1 - (a_{22} + \alpha_2 w_2)$) calls for a concentration of the sectors to one centre. Under conditions of a high value of internal use for sector 2, a comparably high total output is required for sector 2 (and a corresponding high need for input from sector 1) per unit delivered (by sector 2) to sector 1, and to agriculture.

The method illustrated for determining the size and number of centres can only be used with small and specially adjusted problems. The two following sections therefore discuss an alternative method requiring a programming model. The model is used in some numerical examples in 4.4.

4.3. A PROGRAMMING MODEL

The model has two characteristics which should be emphasized. In the first place it makes a distinction between foot-loose sectors and locationally restricted sectors. The locations of foot-loose sectors and their sector outputs in different locations are determined by the model. The model also determines deliveries of goods within the system of centres. Sectors belonging to the second category use specific natural resources, which restrict them to locations where these resources are available. Agriculture and raw material production are among these sectors. The outputs of a restricted sector are assumed to be given on a location and correspond to the capacity of, for example, a coal mine or a given area of arable land. When assuming restricted sectors we have considered the first of Bos's conditions for hierarchy (see 2.1).[8]

The second characteristic of the model is that output in a centre of a foot-loose sector is not allowed to fall below the minimum level where production is feasible in a plant. As economies of scale are taken into consideration, programming models do not become linear. Development within the field of integer programming has shown, however, that the problem can be reformulated as a linear program. See, for example, Abadie (1970). Such a reformulation is realized by variables of 0 or 1.

A number of locations ($h = 1 \ldots H$) are given. These are assumed to be so small that costs for internal transports may be ignored. Because of the integer variables, larger problems are difficult to solve. Consequently, it is the solution algorithm rather than the question at issue that determines the number of possible centres in the model. A weakness of the model is that the number and location of centres must be given. Hereby the programming model is more biased than the model of Lösch (see 2.2.1).

Firstly the model is formulated, and thereafter the objective function and the various constraints are explained. The problem is:

$$\min \sum_h \sum_{h'} \sum_i x_i^{hh'} \, d^{hh'} \, t_i \qquad h \neq h' \qquad (4.11)$$

subject to

$$b_i x_i^h + \sum_{h'} x_i^{h'h} - \sum_{h'} x_i^{hh'} - \sum_{j \neq i} v_{ij} x_j^h \geqq 0 \quad i = 1 \ldots . n \qquad (4.12)$$

$$x_k^h = q_k^h \bar{x}_k \qquad k = 1 \ldots . n' \qquad (4.13)$$

$$x_p^h + (z_p^h - 1)\bar{c}_p \geqq 0 \qquad p = n' + 1 \ldots . n \qquad (4.14)$$

$$-x_p^h - (z_p^h - 1) \, \bar{G}_p \geqq 0 \qquad p = n' + 1 \ldots . n \qquad (4.15)$$

$$z_p^h \text{ either } 0 \text{ or } 1 \qquad (4.16)$$

$$x_i^{hh'} \geqq 0; \, x_p^h \geqq 0$$

Notations:

$x_i^{hh'}$: output of sector i, delivered from centre h to h'. Determined by the model ($h, h' = 1 \ldots . H; i = 1 \ldots . n$)

x_p^h : output of a foot-loose sector p in centre h. Determined by the model ($h = 1 \ldots . H; p = n' + 1, \ldots . n$)

$\bar{x}_p$: total output of a sector p. This is given ($p = n' + 1, \ldots . n$)

x_i^h : output of sector i in centre h.

x_k^h : output of a locationally restricted sector k in centre h ($h = 1 \ldots . H; k = 1 \ldots . n'$)

$\bar{x}_k$: total output of a foot-loose sector k. This is given ($k = 1, \ldots . n'$)

q_k^h : ratio between output of a locationally restricted sector k in h, and total output of the sector. The following condition must hold for each k:

$$\sum_{h=1}^{H} q_k^h = 1$$

The values of these ratios are given.

t_i : cost of transporting one unit of product i one unit of distance.

$d^{hh'}$: distance between centres h and h'.

$\bar{c}_p$: capacity of a plant in sector i. This is given and corresponds to the minimum level where production is at all feasible ($p = n' + 1, \ldots . n$)

a_{ij} : input coefficient of product i in the production process of product j.

β_i : $1 - (a_{ii} + \alpha_i w_i)$.

β_i denotes what is left per unit of output in sector i after the internal use of the sector has been subtracted.

λ_{ij} : $a_{ij} + \alpha_i w_j$ Generalized input-output coefficient.

α_i : coefficient relating final demand for sector i to income. This includes means of subsistence for the workers and their families. $\sum\limits_{i=1}^{n} \alpha_i$ must be fulfilled. The values of these parameters are given.

w_j : ratio between value added and output for sector j.

$\bar{G}_p$: constant that should meet the condition $\bar{G}_p > \bar{x}_p$ ($p = n' + 1 \ldots . n$)

Output of a footloose sector in a centre and the deliveries within the system of centres are determined so as to minimize total transportation costs (4.11). An alternative formulation would be to minimize the sum of transportation and investment costs. An objective function including investments is, however, only meaningful if the centres have different capital-output ratios. In other words (4.11) assumes that the centres lack relative cost advantages. Investment costs are thus assumed to be independent of location choice.

(4.11) has also been formulated so that the model may be used in the micro-phase of stepwise planning (cf. 2.2.3). The task of planning is then to determine the allocation of investments between centres on the basis of an investment plan (investments allocated among sectors) already drawn up during the middle phase. Variations of the capital-output ratio between centres are ignored as they

are assumed to have been taken into consideration during the preceding planning phase.

The given total output for sectors requires a corresponding quantity of investment. Such needs for investments are assumed to
influence the coefficients relating final demand for sectors to income.
This implies that α_i not only considers consumer demand for goods
from sector i, but also includes demand for investment goods.

A centre is a local market. Output and imports must never fall
below local consumption and exports in any sector. This is ensured
(4.12). Out of a total of n sectors, $1 \ldots n'$ are restricted. Output
for these restricted sectors is given in a place (4.13).

Let us leave the model for a while and see what happens when
there is a modification in the use of outputs from restricted sectors?
One assumption which underpins our reasoning is that such changes
have a considerable influence on the system of centres. This is most
evidently shown when the energy and natural resource basis of a
society is changed. Here lies a weakness in our model, since only
restricted sectors preclude total concentration to one large centre.
With the actual formulation of the objective function it would be
preferable to aim at a long-term change in the use of output from
restricted sectors leading to a concentration of all production to only
one centre. This deficiency does not exist in the model presented in
chapter 5 where constraints are applied to the available land in the
centres.

Economies of scale are taken into consideration by (4.14)–
(4.16). How this is done may be shown by introducing the following
type of restrictions:

$$\text{either } G(x_1, x_2 \ldots x_n) \geqq 0$$

$$\text{or else } H(x_1, x_2 \ldots x_n) \geqq 0$$

As an example it is stipulated that the output of sector i in location
h, x_i^h, should fulfill $x_i^h \geqq 1000$ or else $x_i^h = 0$. This can be written
as:

$$\text{either: } x_i^h - 1000 \geqq 0$$

$$\text{or: } -x_i^h \qquad \geqq 0$$

An integer variable, z_p^h, whose value is either 0 or 1, is introduced.

The requirements for convexity of linear programs are then satisfied by the constraints (4.14) − (4.16).

Qualitative requirements of the type 'either – or' have been turned into constraints that are known in standard programming. The only difference is that some of the variables, z_p^h, are either 0 or 1. If $z_p^h = 0$, this implies that the sector is present in centre h and $z_p^h = 1$ implies that the sector is absent.

(4.15) is only efficient when $z_p^h = 1$, that is, in centres where sector p does not have any plant. When z_p^h is zero, there is no need for an upper limit on the output of the sector in a centre h. (4.13) guarantees that the total output of the sector is not exceeded. The only requirement is that $\overline{G}_p$ is greater than $\bar{x}_p$.

(4.14) states that the output of a foot-loose sector in a centre has to be greater than, or equal to, the capacity of the plant. It is impossible to introduce conditions which take into consideration that only entire plants can exist, without complicating the model considerably. It is therefore assumed possible to round off when the output of a foot-loose sector does not exactly correspond to the total capacity of an integer number of plants. If, for example, the output in a centre is so great that 2,5 plants are required, it is assumed that the same output can be attained with two plants.

The model holds for a closed economy. However, it can be adjusted with regard to trade; for example, by assuming that a given share of the total output of the sectors is destined for export. At the same time, it may be assumed that the income, Y, determines the imports. All imports and exports pass through H, which is assumed to have a central position in the communication system. Each sector in (4.12) corresponding to $h = H$ is therefore supplied with exogenously determined quantities, which take into consideration the difference between imports and exports.

The transportation sector is not indicated in the model. Since the transportation system does not deprive the other sectors of any resources, the resource needs of the sector must be satisfied from outside. Optimization then implies that this supply is made as small as possible.

Finally, we will comment on the procedure of optimization. When integer variables occur, the program cannot be solved by standard methods. Instead, algorithms for combinatorial solutions are used.[9] Since the number of possible combinations grows quickly when the number of integer variables increases, a good algorithm should determine optimum, or at least a satisfactory approximation of optimum, without having to investigate all possible solutions. There are $2^{n.H}$ combinations to the problem above. In the numerical examples discussed later, seven places and three sectors with capacity restrictions occur. In other words there are already in this simple case 2^{21} possibilities.[10]

The method of elaborating reliable search procedures varies, but the underlying principle is usually identical. In a supplement to chapter 4 this principle is illustrated by an example from Balas (1967). For one of the calculations in 4.3, OPHELIE MIXTE was used.[11]

4.4. SOME NUMERICAL EXAMPLES

Tinbergen's hypothesis (see 2.2.2) only holds when special conditions are fulfilled. The market areas must be squares, which give higher transportation costs than the systems of Christaller and Lösch, where market areas are hexagonal. Also a programming model, like the one in 4.3, sets out from a lot of preconditions, (for example, that the locations and number of the centres are given) and omits so many aspects, that only some of the properties of an optimal system of centres are brought out. With this reservation, we will pass on to some numerical examples, using the programming model in 4.3.

In the first two numerical examples, output for four foot-loose sectors are determined in seven centres, together with deliveries of products between the centres. The difference between the examples lies in the value of the coefficient relating final demand for agriculture to total income. The third example shows optimum for different spatial distributions of agriculture and raw materials. With these examples we want to study whether a 'perfect' hierarchy (see 2.2.3) corresponds to a system of centres where transportation costs are minimized. This is in no way an exhaustive analysis, the calculations aiming primarily at illustrating a method.

From the beginning, the calculations were meant to be made on the basis of the total input-output table included in the revised version of the Swedish Long Term Surveys for 1970 (SOU 1973.21).

Because of the occurrence of integer variables in the model, it was, however, considered necessary to reduce the number of sectors.

The data basis for the calculations is summarized in tables 4.1–4.4.

Six sectors were used. These were obtained by aggregating the sectors in the Long Term Surveys (see table 4.1).[12] Sector 24 in the Long Term Surveys 'Importation of foreign tourist services', was excluded. This was possible since the input-output coefficients concerned are zero. The input-output matrix is presented in table 4.2.

The number of centres was restricted to seven (table 4.3). In considering accessibility (the total of the distances separating one centre from other centres) three levels can be distinguished. A has the most central position in the whole system, while F and G are superior to B and D, and C and E, respectively. Transportation routes are traced in table 4.3, and the distances between centres are indicated. The calculations should preferably be as realistic as possible. We therefore begin with values of α_i corresponding to the relative importance of the sectors to the Swedish economy. Such values have been determined on the basis of the calculations of the Long Term Surveys for 1970. For each sector, consumption (both private and public) is summarized, as well as gross investments. The values of α_i are obtained by dividing this sum by the income Y. The parameters are presented together with the ratios between value added and output w_i in table 4.4. The freight rates t_i are 1 for all sectors.

In all examples it is assumed that the income, Y, is 10 000. Economies of scale are only taken into consideration for sectors 2–4. Capacities of plants are set in such a way that sector 4 requires 1 plant, sector 3 requires 7, and sector 2 requires 30 plants. An integer algorithm (OPHELIE MIXTE) is only used in the third example.

Table 4.1. Classification of sectors.

Sector rank	Denomination	Corresponding sectors in the Long Term Surveys of 1970
0	Agriculture and fishing	1, 2
00	Extractive industry	3
1	Construction, trade, transport, energy and services	18–23
2	Metal sectors, e.g. manufacturing	14–17
3	Manufacture of food and textiles	4–7
4	Other sectors (except metal sectors), e.g. chemical industry	8–13

Table 4.2. Input-output coefficients.

Delivering sector	Receiving sector 0	00	1	2	3	4
0	0,02634	0	0,00229	0	0,12034	0,03670
00	0,00138	0,05878	0,00466	0,01930	0	0,03423
1	0,25707	0,32626	0,18148	0,23334	0,24510	0,20852
2	0,03869	0,07440	0,04471	0,31587	0,01348	0,03389
3	0,05811	0	0,01368	0,00119	0,17348	0,01962
4	0,08024	0,03311	0,10146	0,06399	0,04312	0,20259

Table 4.3. Spatial assumptions of the numerical examples.

	A	B	C	D	E	F	G	Accessibility
A	—							7,5
B	$\sqrt{2}$	—						11,5
C	$\sqrt{2}$	2	—					11,5
D	$\sqrt{2}$	2	$2\sqrt{2}$	—				11,5
E	$\sqrt{2}$	$2\sqrt{2}$	2	2	—			11,5
F	1	1	$\sqrt{5}$	1	$\sqrt{5}$	—		9,5
G	1	$\sqrt{5}$	1	$\sqrt{5}$	1	2	—	9,5

Table 4.4. Other parametrical assumptions.

Sector	Ratios between value added and output w_i	Coefficients relating final demand to income α_i	Freight rates t_i
0	0,53817	0,03	1
00	0,50745	0,00	1
1	0,65172	0,44	1
2	0,36631	0,18	1
3	0,40448	0,25	1
4	0,46445	0,10	1

The calculations in the other two examples are based on different a priori assumptions concerning the location of those foot-loose sectors which are characterized by economies of scale. For each assumption, the sector outputs in the centres, and deliveries of goods, are determined.

Thereafter, the solutions corresponding to the different assumptions are compared as to the value of the objective function. This procedure makes it impossible to state with certainty whether a solution is optimal. Thus we have to content ourselves with more preliminary statements such as 'a certain system of centres is more favourable than another.'

It is not necessary to make the assumptions totally at random. If the dual variables corresponding to (4.14) are used, one assumption may form the basis of the next one. If the output of a sector in a centre is equal to the minimum level where production is feasible $(\bar{c}_i)$, and the sector also occurs in centres where accessibility is more advantageous, transportation costs probably diminish if the next assumption implies that the sector only occurs in the latter centres. A plant producing at the minimum level where production is feasible is characterized by the dual variable corresponding to (4.14), being differentiated from zero.

A detailed presentation of the calculations is to be found in appendix 4. First, two examples are discussed in which the coefficient relating final demand for agriculture to total income has different values. One of the examples implies that this coefficient is equal to the one presented in table 4.4. In the second example, the importance of the agricultural sector is increased. α_0 is changed from 0,03 to 0,11 and α_2, that is, the coefficient for Metal sectors, diminishes from 0,18 to 0,10. In both examples, the agricultural sector is assumed to be evenly spread among all centres and the Extractive industry is evenly spread between C and D.

We start with the smallest share for agricultural production. Table 4.5 presents two assumed locational alternatives for foot-loose sectors characterized by economies of scale. The crosses show where production for these sectors is assumed to take place. The computations are not complicated by these a priori assumptions. The integer variables corresponding to the crosses in table 4.5 are set at 0 only, while the remaining integer variables are set at 1. The solution is then determined as in a usual linear programming problem.

Table 4.5. A priori assumptions concerning location of some foot-loose sectors, in the example with the smaller coefficient relating final demand for agriculture to income.

Centre	Assumption1			Assumption 2		
	2	3	4	2	3	4
A	x	x	x	x	x	x
F	x	x	—	x	x	—
G	x	x	—	x	x	—
B	x	—	—	—	—	—
C	x	—	—	x	—	—
D	x	—	—	x	—	—
E	x	—	—	—	—	—

The result of the first assumption and the first example is presented in figure 4.2 (see also appendix 4). The cubes represent centres. In the figure, centre A, which has the most advantageous position in the communication system, has been placed on top. Next below are centres F and G, while B, C, D and E, where accessibility is the least favourable, are situated at the very bottom. The figures inside a cube indicated the sector composition of a centre and the arrows denote deliveries. In the latter case, the figures refer to delivering sectors. Furthermore, deliveries for locationally restricted sectors are accounted for separately, in the smaller figure.

The system of centres in figure 4.2 agrees with a 'perfect' hierarchy[13] but for one respect. This concerns two of the smallest centres, B and E, which export metal goods (2) to the larger centres F and G. Centre A is self-sufficient except for agricultural products (0) and goods from the Extractive industry (00). The centre only exports from the highest-ranking sector – sector 4.

The other centres are self-sufficient in agriculture and export their surplus to A. Furthermore, F and G export foodstuffs and textiles (sector 3) to the smaller centres B, C, D and E.

In two cases the dual variables corresponding to (4.14) are differentiated from zero. This concerns sector 2 in B and E. Because of this, a second assumption was made where the sector was absent in these centres. Thus a more favourable structure was obtained (figure 4.3). The value of the objective function diminished from 21,66 to 21,13. Centre A is still self-sufficient, except for commodities from agriculture and from the Extractive industry. However,

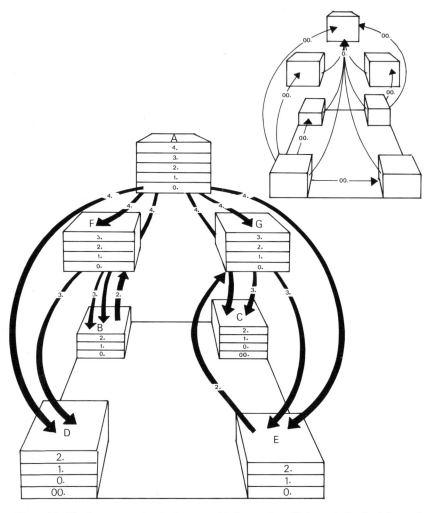

Figure 4.2. The first assumption in the case with the small coefficient relating final demand for agricultural products to income. Value of the objective function: 21.66.

there are not only deliveries from section 4, metal goods are also exported. The latter are directed exclusively towards *B* and *E*. Simultaneously, the needs for metal goods of *B* and *E* are partially satisfied from *F* and *G*. According to Tinbergen, this should lead to a situation where sector 2 is locally balanced in centre *A*.

The deviation from a 'perfect' hierarchy can be interpreted as though optimum has not yet been found. The fact is that the solution leads to a situation where production for sector 3 in *F* and *G*

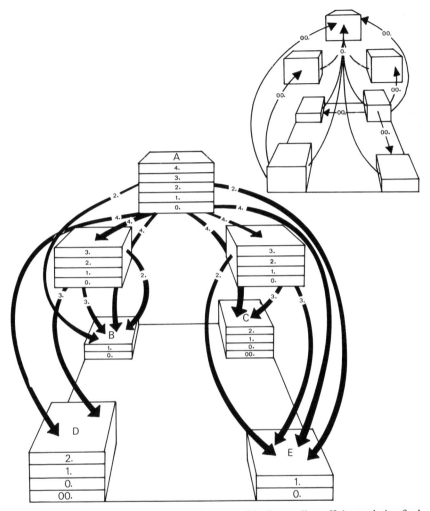

Figure 4.3. The second assumption in the case with the small coefficient relating final demand for agricultural products to income. Value of the objective function: 21.13

takes place at the minimum level where production is feasible (the dual variables corresponding to (4.14) are differentiated from zero).

Since output is equal to the capacity of the plant, transportation costs would probably decrease if the production of sector 3 was fully concentrated to *A*.

Since the second assumption also implies that two of the smallest centres (*B* and *E*), have their needs for metal goods satisfied from *A*, it is possible that the production within sector 2 in *F* and *G* should also be concentrated to A. This would imply that optimum is identical with the special case when all sectors characterized by economies of scale, except sector 2 in C and D, are fully concentrated to A. Unfortunately it has not been possible to investigate whether this alternative leads to a more favourable structure.[14]

The result in figures 4.2–4.3 is compared, in the second example, to a situation where the coefficient relating final demand of agriculture to income is greater. α_0 is therefore changed from 0,03 to 0,11 and α_2 (the coefficient relating final demand for Metal sectors to income) from 0,18 to 0,10. The spatial distribution of the agricultural sector and the Extractive industry is the same as in the example with the smaller coefficient for the agricultural sector.

The structure used in assumption 1 in this example is the same as assumption 1 in the former example (see table 4.5). The system of centres and the value of the objective function are presented in figure 4.4. The system is entirely according to Tinbergen's hypothesis. Centre A is self-sufficient, except for goods from agriculture and from the Extractive industry, which are imported. Only goods from sector 4 are exported from the centre. F and G only import from sector 4 in A and export only from sector 3, and then to the smaller centres B, C, D and E. These, in turn, have a local demand for metal goods, sufficient to make sector 2 locally balanced in these centres.

The first assumption entailed that all dual variables corresponding to (4.14) were zero. Consequently, nothing is stated about which direction to choose when changing the locations of sectors 2–4. In the earlier example, with the smaller agricultural sector, the relocation of sector 2 from B and E to F and G (assumption 2) led to a more favourable system of centres. Thus it seems reasonable to try the same relocation here. In the second assumption no production was therefore allowed for sector 2 in B and E. A less favourable structure was then obtained, however. The value of the objective function increased to 30,19. It is therefore of less interest to discuss this solution in detail.

The result seems to be identical with the result of the simple models in 4.2. In that case too, a large coefficient relating final demand for agricultural products to income indicated a more dispersed spatial structure than a small coefficient.

The system of centres in figure 4.4 probably implies that we have found optimum for the second numerical example. Then the result

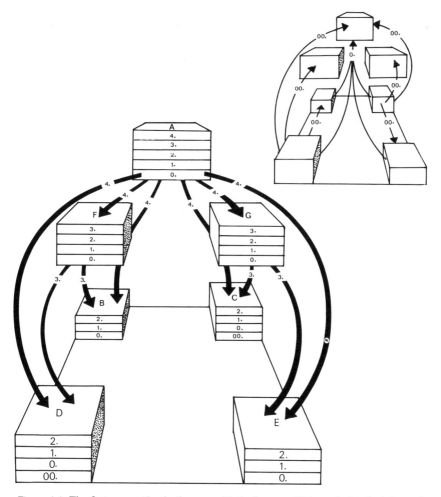

Figure 4.4. The first assumption in the case with the large coefficient relating final demand for agricultural products to income. Value of the objective function: 29.75.

supports Tinbergen's hypothesis about a system of centres where transportation costs are minimized. This is true for input-output coefficients and whith reasonable assumptions concerning proportions between sector outputs.

In the first numerical example, with the smaller coefficient relating final demand for agriculture to income, optimum was difficult to establish. We assumed that optimum implied a system of centres where all sectors characterized by economies of scale were concentrated to *A*. This example is therefore consistent with actual observations, namely that in advanced economies, that is, countries with a small agricultural sector, it is almost impossible to identify sectors that are exclusively local in large centres. In the case of Stockholm this has been shown by Artle (1957, p. 304–305).

We have not yet touched upon the importance of the locations of agriculture and natural resources. One question in this context is whether locations of sectors characterized by economies of scale

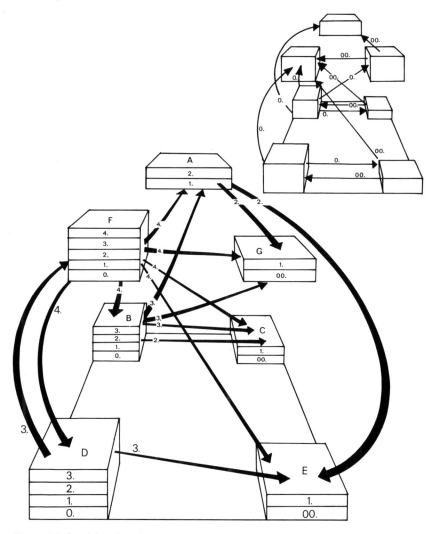

Figure 4.5. Special regions for agriculture and Extractive industry, respectively. Value of the objective function: 18.25.

to several centres are optimal also when the coefficient for agriculture is small. In other words: can a different distribution of the restricted sectors 0 and 00 prevent the concentration to one centre when α_0 is small? This is investigated in the third example, where agriculture (0) only occurs within one of the regions, and Extractive industry (00) in the other. 0 is thus evenly spread between B, F and D, and 00 is distributed in a similar way between C, G and E. Neither 0 nor 00 occur in centre A, the α-values being the same as in table 4.4. In this case nothing was assumed about foot-loose sectors, but optimum was determined with OPHELIE MIXTE (figure 4.5).

What is most striking in this numerical example is that centre A does not become the metropolis.[15] F, the superior centre within the agricultural region, takes this place instead, and assumes the same size and sector composition as A had in the previous examples. The only activity in A, apart from sector 1, is a plant for the production of metal goods. Another difference in comparison with a situation when 0 and 00 are evenly spread is that the concentration to A is replaced by a corresponding concentration to the agricultural region. There is namely no production for sectors 2–4 within the region with Extractive industry. The needs for goods from sectors with economies of scale must therefore be satisfied by imports from the agricultural region and A.

The system of centres in the agricultural region has two geographical levels. In F, all activities, except sector 4, are locally balanced, while B and D are centres of export for sectors 2 and 3. An irregular distribution of agriculture and natural resources therefore seems to prevent the concentration of sectors 2–4 to only one centre, which appeared to be the case in the previous example with the same value for α_0, but with and even distribution of agriculture and Extractive industry.

4.5. PROBLEMS WHEN DECISION-MAKING IS INDIVIDUAL AND
     BASED ON PRICE INFORMATION

4.5.1. Interpretation of the Lagrangean corresponding to the model
After the numerical examples in 4.4, the next question is whether optimum to the model in 4.3 can be maintained when decision-making is individual and based on price information. If this turns out to be impossible, one more question is raised, namely, what

an alternative implementation system would be like. Problems in decentralized decision-making are now discussed on the basis of the Lagrangean corresponding to the model in 4.3.

Methods for solving linear programming problems are sometimes interpreted as the working of the real, everyday market. It is then imagined that the adjustments at market disequilibria resemble the iterations of algorithms when these converge towards optimum and equilibrium. Another interpretation is that the iterations can be regarded as negotiations between planning units. Here it is a problem of preparing decisions (the plan) with no effect on the real working of the economy. Kornai (M. Goreux et al., 1973, p. 527) argues that the latter interpretation is possible. The analogy to market processes is, however, partly misleading, In the market process, states of disequilibrium arise with a surplus of supply and demand, and this starts complicated processes. Among other things, stock-keeping is influenced – something not considered by the solution algorithms. We will discuss a more limited problem. The question concerned is whether the dual prices determined at optimum of the model in 4.3 can be interpreted as a price system for an economy which already is in equilibrium. If single decision-makers are to be in equilibrium, all profits have to be non-positive.

Before discussing characteristics of the dual corresponding to the model (4.13) is inserted into (4.12). From (4.13) the total output of a restricted sector k, situated in centre h, is given. The supply of the sector is thus given (excluding the needs of the other restricted sectors, which are also given). This supply is written $\overline{O}_k^h$. With given total outputs for restricted sectors, it also follows that their total demand for deliveries from a foot-loose sector, p, situated in a centre h, is given ($\overline{I}_{pL}^h$).

$\overline{O}_k^h$ and $\overline{I}_{pL}^h$ are determined:

$$\beta_k q_k^h \overline{x}_k - \sum_{j \neq k} \gamma_{kj} q_j^h \overline{x}_j = \overline{O}_k^h \qquad h = 1 \ldots H$$
$$k = 1 \ldots n' \qquad (4.17)$$

$$\sum_k \gamma_{pk} q_k^h \overline{x}_k = \overline{I}_{pL}^h \qquad h = 1 \ldots H \qquad p = n' + 1 \ldots n \quad (4.18)$$

If (4.17) and (4.18) are inserted into the model, (4.12) falls into two parts. One part (4.19) below, is the conditions for balance of foot-loose sectors, and the other (4.20), is the conditions for balance of restricted sectors:

$$\beta_p x_p^h + \sum_{h'} x_p^{h'h} - \sum_{h'} x_p^{hh'} - \sum_{j \neq p} \gamma_{pj} x_j^h \geq \bar{I}_{pL}^h$$

$$h = 1 \dots H \quad p = n' + 1 \dots n \quad (4.19)$$

$$\bar{O}_k^h + \sum_{h'} x_k^{h'h} - \sum_{h'} x_k^{hh'} - \sum_{p} \gamma_{kp} x_p^h \geq 0$$

$$h = 1 \dots H \qquad k = 1 \dots n' \quad (4.20)$$

In the first two numerical examples in 4.4 the values of the integer variables were given a priori. In the following discussion the same assumption will be made. The problem to be discussed is illustrated in figure 4.6:

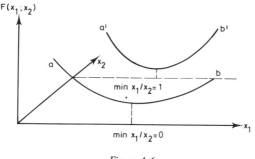

Figure 4.6.

The figure contains one continuous variable, x_1, and one integer variable, x_2. The latter is either zero or one. ab and $a'b'$ indicate the value of the objective function, $F(x_1; x_2)$, for different values of x_1 when x_2 is zero or one, respectively. The treatment is restricted to local optima. The value of x_2 is assumed given and the discussion concerns conditions for a local optimum situated on curves such as ab and $a'b'$. No effort is made, however, to characterize the local optimum which is also global, that is, optimum with regard to both x_1 and x_2. The solution is instead assumed given, and determined on the basis of the method in the supplement to chapter 4. The local optimum discussed below is therefore assumed to be global.

After substituting (4.12) and (4.13) for (4.19) and (4.20), the

Lagrangean corresponding to the model is written:

$$L = \sum_h \sum_{h'} \sum_i x_i^{hh'} d^{hh'} t_i - \sum_h \sum_p u_p^h (\beta_p x_p^h + \sum_{h'} x_p^{h'h} - \sum_{h'} x_p^{hh'} -$$

$$\sum_{j \neq p} \gamma_{pj} x_j^h - \bar{I}_{pL}^h) - \sum_h \sum_k u_k^h (\sum_{h'} x_k^{h'h} - \sum_{h'} x_k^{hh'} - \sum_p \gamma_{kp} x_p^h + \bar{0}_k^h) -$$

$$\sum_h \sum_p t_p^h (x_p^h + z_p^h \bar{c}_p - \bar{c}_p) + \sum_h \sum_p s_p^h (x_p^h + z_p^h \bar{G}_p - \bar{G}_p) \qquad (4.21)$$

Both u_p^h and u_k^h are non-negative. At optimum u_p^h indicates the increase of transportation costs with a marginal increase of the demand of restricted sectors for commodities from a foot-loose sector p in centre h. The second variable, u_k^h, indicates the reduction of transportation costs which follows if the supply from the restricted sector k increases marginally in centre h. u_p^h is interpreted as a price of commodity p in h and u_k^h, in a similar way, as a price of commodity k in h. t_p^h and s_p^h cannot be interpretated as commodity prices, but correspond to our constraints, designed to take economies of scale into consideration. t_p^h and s_p^h are non-negative. We return to the interpretation of these later.

The partial derivative of $x_p^{hh'}$, $x_k^{hh'}$ and x_p^h is now found. The Kuhn-Tucker conditions state that, at a local optimum, the partial derivative with respect to, for example, $x_p^{hh'}$ should be greater than, or equal to, zero (Intrilligator, 1971, p. 51). If the derivative is greater than zero $x_p^{hh'} = 0$. For $x_p^{hh'} > 0$ it is required that the derivative is zero.

The derivative with respect to $x_p^{hh'}$ is:

$$\frac{\delta L}{\delta x_p^{hh'}} = d^{hh'} t_p + u_p^h - u_p^{h'} \geq 0 \qquad (4.22)$$

This condition states that the price of a product p in a centre h', should be less than, or equal to, the price of the product in another centre h, plus transportation costs between the centres. When equality holds any quantity of the product may be delivered from h to h' ($x_p^{hh'} > 0$).

Next:

$$\frac{\delta L}{\delta x_k^{hh'}} = d^{hh'} t_k + u_k^h - u_k^{h'} \geq 0 \qquad (4.23)$$

This condition is interpreted in the same way as (4.22).

Finally, the partial derivative of the output of a foot-loose sector in a centre is found:

$$\frac{\delta L}{\delta x_p^h} = - u_p^h \beta_p + \sum_{i \neq p} u_i^h \gamma_{ip} + (s_p^h - t_p^h) \geqq 0 \qquad (4.24)$$

Thus, the following must hold in a centre h: the price of product p, multiplied by what is left per unit of output after the internal use of the sector has been subtracted, should be less than, or equal to, the cost of inputs from other sectors plus $(s_p^h - t_p^h)$.

t_p^h and s_p^h are discussed on the one hand in cases where a sector p occurs in a centre h ($z_p^h = 0$), and on the other when it is absent in h ($z_p^h = 1$). If sector p is present in h, (4.15) is never efficient (equality never holds) so that s_p^h is always zero. With the same assumption ($z_p^h = 0$) t_p^h can be differentiated from zero only if production takes place at the minimum level of production. Thereby t_p^h can be interpreted as an increase of transportation costs at a marginal increase of the plant capacity of sector p in h. In the second case, that is, when sector p does not have any plant in h, the equalities in (4.14) and (4.15) always hold. Thereby both t_p^h and s_p^h can be differentiated from zero. In this case the variable difference $s_p^h - t_p^h$ is interpreted as an increase ($t_p^h > s_p^h$) or a decrease ($s_p^h > t_p^h$), respectively, of the transportation costs at a marginal production of commodity p in h.

If optimum implies that a sector p should produce in h ($x_p^h > 0$) equality must hold in (4.24). At equality, and if x_p^h is greater than the plant capacity, profits are zero ($u_p^h \beta_p - \sum_{i \neq p} u_i^h \gamma_{ip} = 0$). If, on the contrary, $x_p^h = \bar{c}_p$ and if $t_p^h \neq 0$, a sector p will produce at a loss in a centre h ($u_p^h \beta_p - \sum_{i \neq p} u_i^h \gamma_{ip} = - t_p^h$). Then optimum can only be consistent with equilibrium for the micro-units if sector p situated in h is subsidized by an amount corresponding to t_p^h per unit produced.

If inequality holds in (4.24), a sector p should not have any production in a centre h, that is, the micro-units should lack incentives to start production in h. Such incentives are only lacking when prices, according to optimum, imply that the profits of sector p are non-positive in h ($u_p^h \beta_p - \sum_{i \neq p} u_i^h \gamma_{ip} \leqq 0$).

There are thus two possibilities. If $s_p^h - t_p^h \leqq 0$ profits are always non-positive. In the second case ($s_p^h - t_p^h > 0$) profits can be positive.

Individual decision-making and economic considerations in the public interest do not then coincide. Instead, the micro-units within sector p have incentives to start production in h, though this is not optimal with regard to transportation costs. If optimum is to be maintained in individual decision-making, sector p requires to be taxed in centres where sector p should not have any plant. Taxes are then determined so as to make profits non-positive.

4.5.2. Some further extensions of the model

Serck-Hanssen (1970, p. 96) discusses a model with one restricted sector and with indivisibilities, treating them differently, however, than in the present study. His result agrees with ours, namely that optimum can only be maintained if certain sectors are taxed in centres where it is known a priori that these should not have any plant. Serck-Hanssen also shows that variables corresponding to s_p^h and t_p^h cannot be interpreted as land rents (p. 115).

(4.24) has been derived without indicating fixed costs in the model. Fixed costs have, however, been taken indirectly into account by the integer constraints of the model. It was thereby assumed that average costs diminish with an increase in the scale of plant. At a scale corresponding to the capacity of a plant ($\bar{c}_p$) they have their least value and keep this for outputs bigger than $\bar{c}_p$. When output is less than the capacity of a plant, average costs are on the one hand variable, and on the other, higher than what is the case when output is greater.

(4.24) is based on a marginal change of output. In a centre where sector p, according to optimum, has no plant ($z_p^h = 1$), a marginal increment of production must be produced in a plant producing below the minimum level at which production is feasible. Average costs then become higher than in centres where the capacity is fully exploited. Thus, if fixed costs are taken into consideration, individual decision-making, based on price information, could probably function without taxation. The profits that may arise, according to (4.24), disappear because of high average costs. On the other hand, if investment decisions are made on the basis of a planned production corresponding to the optimal size of a plant the effect of fixed costs always appears after the decision to build a new plant has been taken. If, at the same time, investment calculations are based on given optimum prices the influence from fixed costs cannot change the previous conclusion that certain sectors require to be taxed in some centres if optimum is to be maintained.

Note that no partial derivate of output from restricted sectors (x_k^h) has been defined. Such a derivative does not exist as x_k^h is assumed given. If, however, (4.13) is changed, allowing sector outputs to vary within an interval, decision-making of locationally restricted sectors can also be discussed. The lower limits of the interval, $x_k^h \geq {}^uc_k$, are then motivated by economies of scale due to fixed costs. It is thus assumed that also restricted sectors require a minimum production scale to be efficient. The output of a restricted sector in a centre is also assumed to have an upper limit, $x_k^h \leq {}^\ddot{o}c_k^h$. This is motivated by the fact that the natural resources, which are utilised by the sector, are limited to a place. The situation within agriculture may serve as an example. When agricultural production is extended within a limited area, average costs rise. This is due to poorer and poorer soils being used. In production exceeding a certain scale (${}^\ddot{o}c_k^h$), average costs are assumed to become so high that the incentive for production disappears.

The Lagrangean corresponding to the model in 4.3 (when (4.13) has been modified so as to take the variation of the x_k^h-variables into consideration) is written:

$$L = \sum_h \sum_{h'} \sum_i x_i^{hh'} d^{hh'} t_i - \sum_h \sum_i u_i^h (\beta_i x_i^h + \sum_{h'} x_i^{h'h} - \sum_h x_i^{hh'} -$$

$$- \sum_{i \neq j} \gamma_{ij} x_j^h) - \sum_h \sum_k {}^uv_k^h (x_k^h - {}^uc_k) + \sum_h \sum_k {}^\ddot{o}v_k^h (x_k^h - {}^\ddot{o}c_k^h) -$$

$$- \sum_h \sum_p t_p^h (x_p^h + z_p^h \bar{c}_p - \bar{c}_p) + \sum_h \sum_p s_p^h (x_p^h + z_p^h \overline{G}_p - \overline{G}_p)$$

u_i^h, ${}^uv_k^h$, ${}^\ddot{o}v_k^h$, t_p^h and s_p^h are all greater than, or equal to, zero. u_i^h is interpreted as the price of a good i when produced in a centre h. t_p^h and s_p^h have the same meaning as in the previous discussion. ${}^uv_k^h$ indicates how much total transportation costs increase with a marginal rise of the lower capacity limit (${}^uc_k$) of a restricted sector k, when the sector is located in h. ${}^\ddot{o}v_k^h$ reflects the decrease of transportation costs with a marginal increase of the upper capacity limit (${}^\ddot{o}c_k^h$) of the section in a centre h.

The partial derivative of x_k^h is defined:

$$\frac{\partial L}{\partial x_k^h} = - u_k^h \beta_k + \sum_{i \neq k} u_i^h \gamma_{ik} - {}^uv_k^h + {}^\ddot{o}v_k^h \geq 0$$

According to the Kuhn-Tucker conditions, equality must hold if $x_k^h \geq 0$. Stability for the micro-units must furthermore imply that profits are zero ($u_k^h \beta_k - \sum_{i \neq k} u_i^h \gamma_{ik} = 0$). When $^u v_k^h$ and $^{\ddot{o}} v_k^h$ are zero, that is when $^u c_k < x_k^h < {}^{\ddot{o}} c_k^h$, this condition is always fulfilled. In the boundary case where $x_k^h = {}^u c_k$, $^u v_k^h \neq 0$ and $u_k^h \beta_k - \sum_{i \neq k} u_i^h \gamma_{ik} = -{}^u v_k^h$.

If optimum implies that a restricted sector k should produce at the lower capacity limit, an implementation system based on price information may give negative profits. The sector must then obtain a subsidy corresponding to $^u v_k^h$ per unit of goods produced if production at optimum is to be consistent with individual decision-making. In the boundary case $x_k^h = {}^{\ddot{o}} c_k^h$, $^{\ddot{o}} v_k^h \neq 0$ is possible. That $^{\ddot{o}} v_k^h$ is differentiated from zero indicates that the natural resource used by sector k in h is scarce, so that $^{\ddot{o}} v_k^h$ can be interpreted as a price of the natural resource. This implies that production at the upper capacity limit gives zero profits and thereby leads to stability for the micro-units ($u_k^h \beta_k - \sum_{j \neq k} u_i^h \gamma_{ik} - {}^{\ddot{o}} v_k^h = 0$).

4.5.3. Some comments on the result

In 4.1 it was shown by an example from Serck-Hanssen that dependencies between producers, in connection with individual decision-making based on prices, may lead to centres which contain more activities than what is optimal with regard to transportation costs. Within a certain size interval of a centre, an individual decision-maker lacked incentives to move out of the centre. To a planning unit, however, a splitting up of the centre into two smaller centres was desirable. It is now possible to state that the model in 4.3 also leads to an optimum, which may be difficult to maintain when decision-making is individual and based on prices. Under such conditions an optimal system of centres (optimal with regard to transportation costs) can, however, be maintained, if certain sectors are taxed in some of the centres. Moreover, in certain cases it is necessary to subsidize parts of the production of a centre.

The following example illustrates the role of taxation.

Let us assume an economy with H manufactured commodities and agriculture. Each process in the manufacture of commodities delivers one unit of output to each one of the other $H–1$ processes. Moreover, manufacturing requires inputs from agriculture. However, there are no deliveries to agriculture.[16]

It is also assumed that manufacturing is divided between two plants. Economies of scale require that K commodities are to be produced in one of them and the remaining H-K commodities in the other plant. Alternatively we may assume that each of the H commodities is produced in a separate factory and that economies of scale are determined by an agglomeration factor, which gives cost advantages if manufacturing is located together into two complexes with K factories in one, and H-K factories in the other.

There are two possible locations for manufacturing – centre 1 and centre 2. Optimum, which is assumed to be determined on the basis of the model in 4.3, is supposed to imply that the cluster containing H-K commodities is to be located to centre 1 and the other cluster (the remaining K commodities) to centre 2. Such a location presumes that both centres have a small agricultural surplus.[17] This implies that prices of products from agriculture are zero in both centres and that there are no deliveries of agricultural products between the centres. However, the surpluses are not large enough to satisfy the total need of industrial production for agricultural products from a single location. This means that, if manufacturing is concentrated to one centre, agricultural products must be transported from the other centre. If the proposed locations are to correspond to optimum, these transportation costs must exceed transportation costs for exchange between factories (when K of these are situated in one of the centres and H-K in the other).

There is a system of prices corresponding to optimum. Since the optimal solution is known, prices are given. Thus the price of agricultural products is zero in both centres. The H-K commodities, which are manufactured in centre 1, are assumed to have identical prices. The price is $\hat{u}_{H\text{-}K}^{1}$.

According to (4.22) the price in the other centre is then $\hat{u}_{H\text{-}K}^{1} + t$, where t indicates the cost of transporting one product unit between the centres. The K commodities, which are manufactured in centre 2, are also assumed to have identical prices at the place of production. This price is $\hat{u}_{k}^{2}$, and the price of the same commodity in centre 1 is $\hat{u}_{k}^{2} + t$.

Let us select one of the K commodities produced in centre 2. This commodity is called k'. We now proceed to discuss the conditions that are necessary if decentralized decisions are to create incentives for producing k' in centre 1, even though this is not optimal.

It is assumed that the production of k' in centre 2 does not take place at the minimum level of production. According to (4.24) marginal returns are then zero in this centre. Marginal returns in centre 1 are:

$$\pi_{k'}^1 = \hat{u}_k^2 + t - \frac{K-1}{H-1}(\hat{u}_k^2 + t) - \frac{H-K}{H-1}\hat{u}_{H-K}^1$$

Marginal returns in centre 2 are zero, that is:

$$\pi_{k'}^2 = \hat{u}_k^2 - \frac{K-1}{H-1}\hat{u}_k^2 - \frac{H-K}{H-1}(\hat{u}_{H-K}^1 + t) = 0$$

After insertion of $\pi_{k'}^2$, we obtain:

$$\pi_{k'}^1 = t\left[1 + \frac{1}{H-1}(H + 1 - 2K)\right] \tag{4.27}$$

$\pi_{k'}^1$ is greater than zero for all possible values of K. With decentralized decisions there are always incentives to produce k' in centre 1 (on condition that K lies in the interval of $1 \leq k < H$). Establishments may be prevented if the production is taxed by an amount corresponding to $\pi_{k'}^1$ per unit of goods. If optimum implies that at least one factory (or one commodity) is to be located in centre 2 (4.27) shows that decentralized decisions, based on price information, can lead to centres with more activities than what is optimal with regard to transportation costs. If optimum is to be maintained in individual decision-making, the K commodities produced in centre 2 require to be taxed if they are produced in the other centre. In a similar way, the other H-K commodities require to be taxed if they are produced in centre 2.

If we also take into consideration the fact that fixed costs can be higher in a centre where a sector should not have any production (according to optimum), the conclusion above must be modified. The higher costs are then due to the fact that production falls below the capacity of the plant, or that economies of agglomeration are lost. Under these circumstances it is possible that the price system could function without taxation, that is, the attractiveness of the centre decreases automatically. This does not hold to the same degree for large centres, since marginal profit, $\pi_{k'}^1$ increases when K decreases. Consequently, it is primarily when centre 1 is large in relation to the second centre that a taxation of k' may become necessary. The example shows that a market mechanism tends to make large centres contain more activities than what is optimal (with respect to transportation costs).

In conclusion, decentralized decisions based on price information are generally incompatible with an optimal system of centres, when optimum is determined by the model in 4.3. In this model a distinction is made between locationally restricted sectors and foot-loose sectors. Furthermore, indivisibilities as well as input-output coefficients are taken into consideration. The results that have been obtained show that a system of centres where transportation costs are minimized is only consistent with decentralized decisions when central planning organs exist simultaneously. Such organs should be aware of optimum and also perform the following functions:

1. Subsidize restricted sectors in centres where optimum leads to production at the minimum level at which production is feasible in a plant. Such a minimum level is motivated by economies of scale and fixed costs.
2. Tax foot-loose sectors in some centres where, according to optimum, they should not have any plant.
3. Subsidize foot-loose sectors in centres where optimum leads to production at the minimum level at which production is feasible in a plant, that is, where sector outputs correspond to plant capacities.

Supplement

BALAS' METHOD FOR COMBINATORIAL SOLUTION OF
INTEGER PROBLEMS

The method of elaborating reliable search procedures in combinatorial solution of integer problems varies, but the underlying principle is usually the same. This is shown by an example (E. Balas, 1967). Balas assumes that n 0–1 variables are given, so that the set of all possible solutions can be divided into n + 1 subsets. Such a set, k (k = 0, 1 . . . n), contains all solutions where k of the integer variables is 1. This implies that the first subset has only one solution and that this corresponds to optimum of an ordinary program, that is, without integer constraints. To begin with, the problem is thus solved continuously. If the continuous solution happens to be feasible with regard to all integer constraints, this is the optimal solution.

As a rule, the continuous solution is not feasible (integer con-

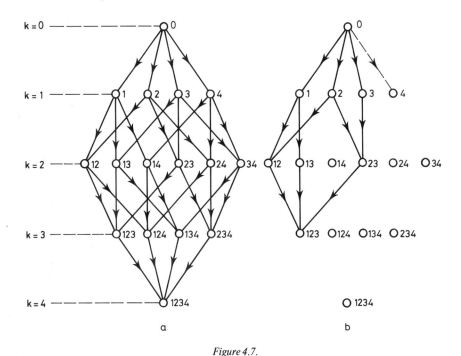

a

b

Figure 4.7.

straints are not met). We then proceed to $k = 1, 2 \dots n$ etc. Figure 4.7 shows the graph of a problem where $n = 4$. The task of the algorithm is to 'cut out' a part of the graph. Having examined the solution in node 0, there are rules for determining which of the variables in $k = 1$ that is to be given the value 1. Each time a node has been explored, the algorithm computes the probability of finding a better solution by proceeding from the node and following one of the arrows downwards to nodes with higher values of k. If the probability is low, the algorithm returns to the next previous node and seeks a new way.

If the first non-continuous solution ($k = 1$) implies that the first variable is set at 1, that is node 1 is sought out, there are rules estimating whether the objective function has a more advantageous value by proceeding to one of the nodes 12, 13 or 14. 123, 124, 134 and 1234 are also considered before the algorithm makes the choice. When there do not appear to be any better values of the objective function, the algorithm returns to node 0 and goes from there to either 2, 3 or 4.

Balas' procedure is such that, when a node is abandoned, the algorithm never returns. If, for example, node 4 in 4.7 is abandoned, then half of all the nodes are also excluded from any further investigation: 14, 24, 34, 124, 134, 234, 1234.

It is evidently decisive what happens to small values of k. An algorithm that makes the 'right choice' from the beginning can both reduce the calculations, and increase the precision. Once the problems are structured, there is much to win in proposing search procedures that are adapted to the character of the problem. The data program, OPHELIE MIXTE, used in 4.4, has properties allowing those who use it to set the rules for guiding the calculations.

NOTES

1. Stuart (1975) emphasizes another reason for this phenomenon: When retailers locate next to each other, this is in order to cut down "consumer costs for information about prices, qualities etc." This produces an effect on the income of consumers that has a favourable influence on retailer profits.
2. The figure is my own.
3. A correct measure for the evaluation of economies of scale of cities should be based on (4.2). Generally, evaluations are based on (4.1), which in some cases leads to an overestimation of the productivity of big cities.
4. Or between the agricultural sector and a centre.

5. Raw material production is fully comparable to agriculture in this respect.
6. The condition is not sufficient to reduce transportation costs in the case of a concentration.
7. Note that (4.9′) and (4.10′) lack magnitudes other than parameters. Serck-Hanssen (1970) uses similar expressions, but the inequalities also contain mangitudes for the outputs of the sectors.
8. A type of activity widely noticed during recent years is polluting industry. This includes pulp factories, nuclear power plants and the petro-chemical industry, all of which consume great quantities of water. Great supplies of water are therefore necessary for these establishments. In the interest of environment, exploitation of such resources has been concentrated to a small number of locations. These two circumstances have made that polluting industry also comes into the locationally restricted category.
9. Two known approaches exist. Either Gomory-constraints (E. M. Beale, 1965) or 'Branch and bound' (N. Agin, 1966) are used. Only the latter method is of interest here.
10. If a computer needs one second to calculate the solution of each combination, it would need, in total, 25 days and nights to compute all combinations.
11. A presentation of OPHELIE MIXTE is found in B. Roy, R. Benayoun, J. Tergny: From SEP procedure to the MIXED OPHELIE (J. Abadie, 1970).
12. The coefficients in the input-output table of the Swedish Long Term Surveys have been summarized by row according to the classification in table 4.1. The totals have been divided by the number of sectors in the respective aggregate. The coefficients in table 4.1 have therefore been obtained by summarizing by column.
13. Tinbergen's hypothesis.
14. Finances did not permit the realization of such a project.
15. It may surprise the reader that no agricultural production or Extractive industry is allowed in A. The explanation is that we expected centre A to become the metropolis in this example too, and that we were interested in studying the inflauence of the absence of agriculture in A on the degree of self-sufficiency for the centre.
16. This assumption is unrealistic, but allows for a certain simplification of the presentation.
17. This implies that we give up the requirements for equality in (4.13).

5. The system of centres when capacities of plants are not given – a further extension of the problem

5.1. PRESENTATION OF THE PROBLEM

Spatial concentration may be considered from two points of view:

1. Spatial concentration when capacities of plants are given
The number of plants are given and the industrial composition of the centres is determined by other factors than those determining capacities of plants. Up to now only this approach has been dealt with.

In 4.4 two examples were discussed where optimal systems of centres were compared for alternative coefficients relating final demand for agriculture to income. In a third example, optimum was investigated for different patterns of location of restricted sectors. The coordination of micro-units also seems to be of importance. The model in 4.3 indicates that an implementation system based on individual decision-making and price information has a tendency to lead to large centres having more activities than is optimal from the transportation cost point of view.

2. Spatial concentration when capacities of plants are variable
The size distribution of plants is sometimes illustrated by a skewed distribution function (cf. 1.1). Irrespective of whether it is single sectors or the industry as a whole that is the subject of study, the x per cent largest plants generally control more than x per cent of the activity (Hjalmarsson, 1974).

The discussion in chapter 4 is now extended to determine capacities of plants and systems of centres simultaneously. This can be realized since the objective function of the model presented in 5.3 also includes fixed costs. Furthermore, the model considers input-output coefficients and economies of scale. Locationally restricted sectors are absent in the model. The first condition for hierarchy in 2.1 has instead been replaced by conditions implying that supplies of land in a centre are limited.

Depending on the degree of complexity, the treatment will be of a more superficial nature than before. The purpose of this chapter is therefore mainly to indicate some possibilities for further research on the relations between size distributions of centres and size distributions of plants indicated in 1.1.

Stochastic models have often served as instruments to explain the size distribution of plants (Simon and Bonini, 1958), (Hymer and Pashigan, 1962), (Mansfield, 1962). In their simplest form, such models are based on the following assumption:

The percentage change in size of plants (firms) in a given size class and during a certain period of time is the same for all size classes.

Hjalmarsson (1974) suggests another approach. Instead of using a stochastic model he tries to explain the existing plant structure in terms of a dynamic production and cost theory. In the model it is assumed that a plant is worn out when the quasi-rent is zero. Furthermore consumption is assumed to grow at a constant geometric rate and production is characterized by economies of scale. Furthermore, the prices of a unit of capital and a current factor are assumed to increase by a given percentage for each period of time. This percentage is different for the factors. The horizon is infinite and there is no uncertainty. It is assumed that the investers decide according to the rule that discounted costs should be minimized.

It is shown by Hjalmarsson that the distribution of plant sizes generated by the model tends to be of the skewed type. If, however, Hjalmarsson had assumed an arithmetical increase of demand, all plants would have been of equal size (cf. Ribrant's result, 1970).

Neither Hjalmarsson nor those who make use of the stochastic model take note of the spatial influence on capacities of plants. The assumption that geographical conditions have an effect is supported by Bain (1966). Bain's investigation comprises eight countries and more than thirty sectors in each country. Plant size has been defined for each sector as an average of the number of workers employed in the twenty largest plants. Bain finds important differences: the United States and England possess the largest average plant sizes while Canada and Sweden have the smallest (p. 39).

Bain claims that there are no simple interpretations of the differences, but that several factors may have an effect, namely, degree of industrialization, population and geographical conditions (p. 40).

It will now be demonstrated how the transportation cost function can be treated in determining the optimal size of a plant. It is thereby assumed that the cost curve of a plant can be defined as the sum of transportation and production costs. It is thus possible to determine the size of a plant producing at minimum cost according to figure 5.1.[1]

Average transportation costs increase and average production costs decrease when the scale of production is extended. The size of a plant producing at minimum costs is then determined where the marginal change of average costs (absolute values) is the same for both categories of costs.

In countries where the population is spread over a large area, the marginal change in average transportation costs should, as a rule, be greater than in densely populated countries. The optimal size of a plant will then be smaller (see figure 5.1). Bains's result, that the average plant size for Sweden and Canada is only 13 and 28 per cent, respectively, of the average for the United States, can probably to some extent be explained by the fact that the former countries are sparsely populated.

Characteristics of the market institution have been discussed earlier, in particular the role of prices in location decisions. From now on we will also take up the possible influence of the market

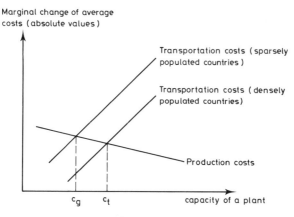

Marginal change of average
costs (absolute values)

Transportation costs (sparsely
populated countries)

Transportation costs (densely
populated countries)

Production costs

c_g c_t capacity of a plant

Figure 5.1.

institution on the size distribution of plants. In this case it is a question of whether a price mechanism is a more profitable allocator of resources than other transaction system.

All economies based on division of labour presuppose cooperation between individuals – in exchange of goods or in production. Usually, economists only study that cooperation which is based on markets. This viewpoint neglects, however, the way in which resources are allocated within systems of transaction other than markets, for example, systems for supervision within a plant. The use of such a system is also accompanied by costs.

In 5.2, control and co-ordination costs will be discussed. The first type of costs represent a utilization of resources defined by the supervision of work within plants. The second type is defined by characteristics of the market institution. Both types of costs enter into the objective function of the programming model presented in 5.3. Together with transportation costs and fixed costs they thus contribute to a simultaneous determination of the system of centres and the size of plants.

5.2. CONTROL AND CO-ORDINATION COSTS

Each plant is assumed to have a contractual agent. The agent buys inputs which are combined to outputs. Outputs are sold as intermediate products, consumption or investment goods. It is of interest how the agent handles these tasks. Before discussing this, all functions performed by the agent, such as supervision of the labour force, collection of information, book-keeping etc, are brought together into one system for the activity within a plant – *the control system* – and into another system for the relations between agents – *the co-ordination system.*

Firstly, a general formula for transformations in regulation systems will be presented. The formula, which comes from Lange (1970), is subsequently used to illustrate the function of the control system. Our starting-point is a regulated system, S. When plants are discussed, all physical capital (machines, intermediate products, raw materials etc) is included in S. The state of output of S is introduced as the input of a governor R which transforms it into its state of output Δx. The state of output of the governor is added to the value of input x of the system S. This kind of 'reversed' influence is called feedback between the activity of governor R and the regulated system S. The coupling may be represented graphically in the form of a block diagram (figure 5.2a).

The feedback of the governor is superimposed upon the input of S, which explains the plus sign in the figure. The effect of R upon S is $\triangle x = Ry$. With this in mind, the output of S may be written as[2]

$$y = S(x + \triangle x) = S(x + Ry) = Sx + SRy$$

Finally, the following relationship between input and output is obtained:

$$y = \frac{S}{1 - SR} x$$

This is a general formula which will now be used to characterize the production within a plant. S thereby denotes a technical relationship with a mechanical structure. R, on the other hand, is a social mechanism, created as a means for man to control the activity in S. In the problem under presentation, R is assumed to correspond to the control system.

The agent has a given quantity of labour (L) at his disposal during a definite, contracted period of time. The only contractual obligation is a lower limit for the amount of work to be executed during the period. We call this the minimum effort of work (m). Above this there is a variable part represented by the control system (R), whose contribution to the effort of work is assumed dependent on the incentives within the control system (figure 5.2b).

According to a theorem that states that the operator corresponding to the serial coupling of two elements equals the product of the operators of these elements (O.Lange, 1970, p. 42), the

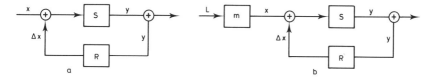

Figure 5.2.

relation between L and y may be written:

$$y = \frac{mS}{1 - SR} L \qquad (5.2)$$

The operator $\left(\dfrac{mS}{1 - SR} \right)$ is a measure of the productivity in a plant. It includes three components: one where technical characteristics predominate and two that are institutionally based (m and R). What is primarily interesting are the characteristics of R, that is, the variable part of the work. This part has been noted earlier, by Vanek (1970, p. 237), among others. He claims that those gains obtainable due to the effort to work being a variable are considerably greater than potential gains from efficient factor combinations.

The variable part of work is assumed to be influenced by the exactitude of the control system (R) in isolating and at the same time measuring individual performance.[3] The reason for this is that individual workers are paid in accordance with their performance and that performance is correlated with reward.

Manuals in economics teach that real wages and productivity of work become equal. It is thereby assumed that some kind of mechanism exists, for example, a market or a type of reward system within an enterprise, that is capable of distributing factor incomes in relation to the productivity of the factors. The problem of identifying and measuring performances is thus ignored. It is always taken for granted that R can correlate reward and performance.

The programming model in the next section assumes that difficulties in identifying and measuring individual performance are greater the larger the plant. It is therefore assumed that R has a tendency to decrease when plant capacity increases.[4] This implies that the operator in (5.2), that is, productivity of work, decreases when there is an increase in scale. If, for example, $R = 0$, (5.2) shows that the variable part of the work disappears altogether. Only the contracted minimum level of work (m) is fulfilled. Because of the metering problem, labour must increase proportionally more than the scale of production (since the operator in (5.2) decreases when y increases, L must increase proportionally more than y), that is average wage costs increase with the size of plant. It is assumed that the fixed capital has no scale effects on wage costs. Costs exclusively dependent on characteristics of the control system are called *control costs*. We will discuss the co-ordination system whose function it is to co-ordinate agents acting within the same sector. In an economy without central planning, the costs for keeping the co-ordination system going are due to characteristics of the market institution. Coase (1937) asks why firms appear at all in a market economy. According to him this is due to the 'cost' of using the market. Contracts must be renewed and prices and product qualities changed continuously, a process accompanied by costs for the agents. According to Coase's reasoning, such costs can be cut down if several agents merge.

Let us show with an example how costs decrease if transactions are pooled through one agent. The example involves costs for establishing relations between seller and buyer. If the number of buyers in a marekt is m, and the number of sellers is n, the total costs of contacts are:

$$K = mnt$$

where t denotes a cost for each contact. If all sellers join together so that all transactions are pooled through one agent, the number of contacts is instead $m + n$, so that the potential profit of a combination may be written as:

$$V = \left[mn - (m + n) \right] t$$

V is positive when m and n are greater than 2 (Baligh and Richartz, 1964).

It is probable that the possibilities of maintaining efficient factor combinations are also influenced by the number of agents. Both perfect competition and monopoly lead to a situation where the agents are independent of one another. In monopoly this is self-evident, and in perfect competition it is the result of the incapacity of an individual agent to influence the activities of other agents. As soon as these extremes give place to more realistic cases, the agents are no longer independent of each other. Under such conditions production corresponding to minimum costs implies that the activities of competitors have to be correctly anticipated.

Co-ordination costs are now introduced and represent costs for maintaining the co-ordination system. It is reasonable that firms try to make these costs as small as possible, for example, by reducing the number of agents. It is also assumed that co-ordination costs can be influenced by the choice of location. This has been observed in some cases where it has been said that firms make themselves independent of their competitors by establishing quasi-monopolies within limited geographical areas. This is why Hotelling's equilibrium of location in duopoly (see 4.1) is not very realistic. With co-ordination costs it is, for example, not very probable that both agents locate next to each other, as such a strategy would result in a continuous change of production plans due to changes in an uncertain market.

Instead, we assume that the agents would try to locate away from each other to escape risk situations and high co-ordination costs. The way co-ordination costs are indicated in our programming model (see 5.3), they have a tendency to restrict the number of agents (plants) while increasing at the same time the distance between the agents within a sector. Like control costs, the latter influence of co-ordination costs has a decentralizing effect upon the geographical structure in the model, while the former influence of co-ordination costs has a centralizing effect upon the geographical structure.

5.3. A MODEL FOR QUADRATIC PROGRAMMING

A programming model is presented which includes four types of costs. Our model has certain similarities with the models of Koopmans and Beckman (1957), or Andersson (1972).

The first type of costs concerns fixed costs. These are assumed to be based on efficient factor combinations, and are supposed to vary with the scale of a plant.[5] Economies of scale are taken into consideration in so far as average fixed costs for a plant are assumed to decrease as the scale increases. This implies that total fixed costs are least when there is only one plant for each sector. Furthermore, total output of a sector in a centre is assumed to be located to one plant.[6] The locations of the centres $h = 1 \ldots H$ are given.

Total fixed costs for a sector i are:

$$f_i = k_i \sum_h \sum_{h'} x_i^h x_i^{h'} \quad h \neq h' \quad i = 1 \dots n \tag{5.3}$$

and

$$\sum_h x_i^h = \bar{x}_i$$

where

x_i^h, $x_i^{b'}$ total output of sector i situated in h and h', respectively.

k_i a constant characterizing the production technique in a plant belonging to sector i.

$\bar{x}_i$ total output of sector i, which is assumed to be given.

When the total output of sector i is concentrated to one plant, (5.3) shows that $f_i = 0$. Fixed costs in this particular case are thus not included in the objective function.

$$\sum_h x_i^h = \bar{x}_i$$

is inserted into (5.3):

$$f_i = k_i \sum_h x_i^h (\bar{x}_i - x_i^h) = k_i \left[\bar{x}_i^2 - \sum_h (x_i^h)^2 \right]$$

The total differential of f_i is:

$$df_i = -2 k_i \sum_h x_i^h \, dx_i^h = 2 k_i \sum_h (\bar{x}_i - x_i^h) \, dx_i^h - 2 k_i \bar{x}_i \sum_h dx_i^h$$

Since the total output of a sector is given, $\sum_h dx_i^h = 0$ must hold, that is

$$df_i = 2 k_i \sum_h (\bar{x}_i - x_i^h) \, dx_i^h \tag{5.4}$$

The share of total output in sector i, produced in a plant situated in centre h is written p_i^h. p_i^h can be interpreted as a measure of concentration. p_i^h is inserted into (5.4):

$$df_i = 2\,k_i\,\bar{x}_i^2 \sum_h (1 - p_i^h)\,dp_i^h$$

Finally, the marginal cost of a change in the scale of production of the plant in centre h is:

$$\frac{\partial f_i}{\partial p_i^h} = 2\,k_i\,\bar{x}_i^2\,(1 - p_i^h) \tag{5.5}$$

This derivative is always greater than, or equal to, zero. (5.5) also shows that the marginal costs of investments decrease when the scale of the plant increases in h, and is zero in $p_i^h = 1$. This implies that the average fixed costs decrease, and attain minimum when the total output of the sector is concentrated to the plant in centre h.

The second type of costs comprises outlays for transports. In previous chapters transportation costs were determined so that all deliveries occur between plants most favourably situated in relation to one another. Subsequently, it is assumed that an agent distributes his purchases among all sellers in a sector. The purchases are assumed proportional to each seller's share of the total sector output. This assumption implies that the optimum of the model allows a commodity to be sent in both directions between two centres ('cross-hauling'). Thus there are other solutions with lower transportation costs. In reality, however, a commodity that is exported from a centre is generally also imported to the same centre. Such solutions are, however, impossible to obtain with linear models. Thus the quadratic model probably has a greater explanatory value than the programming model presented in the previous chapter.

The transportation cost for deliveries between sectors i and j situated in h and h', respectively, is written:

$$tp_{ij}^{hh'} = x_i^h \frac{y_{ij}}{\bar{x}_i} d^{hh'} x_j^{h'} \quad h \neq h' \; h, h' = 1 \ldots . H \; i, j = 1 \ldots . n \tag{5.6}$$

where

$tp_{ij}^{hh'}$ = cost for deliveries from sector i, when it is situated in h, to sector j, when located in h'.

γ_{ij} = generalized input-output coefficient for deliveries from sector i to sector j.

$d^{hh'}$ = cost for delivering one unit of output between h and h'.

We will now indicate control and co-ordination costs in the model. In 5.2 it was assumed that control costs increase when the scale of a plant increases. Since a sector only has one plant in a centre, control costs of a sector are assumed dependent on the output of that sector in the centre.

Control costs for the plant of sector i in h are:

$$kk_i^h = b_i (x_i^h)^2 \quad h = 1 \ldots H \quad i = 1 \ldots n \tag{5.7}$$

where

kk_i^h = control costs for the plant of sector i in h.

b_i = parameter expressing properties of the control system of sector i.

Co-ordination costs have earlier been assumed dependent on the distance to other agents within the same sector.[7] More precisely, the co-ordination cost of an agent is determined partly by the proper output and partly by the total output of the other agents within the same sector. Thereby individual outputs are weighted with respect to the distance between agents. The distance factor is assumed to diminish with increase of distance.

The co-ordination cost for the plant of sector i in h is written:

$$ko_i^h = x_i^h \sum_{h'} b_i^{hh'} x_i^{h'} h \neq h' \quad h = 1 \ldots H \quad i = 1 \ldots n \tag{5.8}$$

where

$b_i^{hh'}$ = parameter partly expressing characteristics of the co-ordination system of sector i, and partly considering the distance between centres h and h'.

Having presented the different types of costs, we will now formulate the model in a case with two centres and two sectors. A quadratic objective function is set up, where the first matrix includes parameters for fixed costs and transportation costs. Parameters for control and coordination costs are included in the second matrix:

$$\min\ (x_1^1, x_2^1, x_1^2, x_2^2) \begin{bmatrix} 0 & 0 & k_1 & z_{12}^{12} \\ 0 & 0 & z_{21}^{12} & k_2 \\ k_1 & z_{12}^{21} & 0 & 0 \\ z_{21}^{21} & k_2 & 0 & 0 \end{bmatrix} \begin{bmatrix} x_1^1 \\ x_2^1 \\ x_1^2 \\ x_2^2 \end{bmatrix} +$$

$$+ (x_1^1, x_2^1, x_1^2, x_2^2) \begin{bmatrix} b_1 & 0 & b_1^{12} & 0 \\ 0 & b_2 & 0 & b_2^{12} \\ b_1^{21} & 0 & b_1 & 0 \\ 0 & b_2^{21} & 0 & b_2 \end{bmatrix} \begin{bmatrix} x_1^1 \\ x_2^1 \\ x_1^2 \\ x_2^2 \end{bmatrix}$$

where

$$z_{ij}^{hh'} = \frac{\gamma_{ij}}{x_i}\, d^{hh'} \text{ in } (5.6)$$

The objective function is minimized subject to:

$$\sum_{h=1}^{2} x_i^h = \bar{x}_i\ i = 1, 2$$

$$\sum_{i=1}^{2} e_i\, x_i^h \leq f^h\ h = 1, 2$$

$$x_i^h \geq 0$$

The first condition implies that the total output of a sector, summarized for the centres, should be equal to a given total sector output. Locationally restricted sectors are absent in the model. The first condition of hierarchy in 2.1 has therefore been replaced by conditions implying a limitation of available land in a centre – the second condition above. Furthermore, the model contains both indivisibilities and input-output coefficients. We will subsequently discuss whether the problem is convex. If convex, Kuhn-Tucker's theory may be used to determine conditions for stability of a global optimum when decisions are made individually and based on price information. To achieve stability, all profits must be non-positive.

In the general case, with n sectors and H centres, the model is:[8])

(5.9) min $x \, Q \, x^T = x \, G \, x^T + x \, K \, x^T$

subject to

$$Ax^T = \bar{x}^T$$

$$Ex^T \leqq f^T$$

$$x^T \geqq 0$$

The matrices of the objective function are of the nxH^{th} order. For convexity Q has to be positive semidefinite (Andersson, 1972). This implies, that the diagonal elements in Q should be great in relation to other elements in the matrix. Since all diagonal elements in G have the value zero, convexity never holds if the model only includes fixed costs and transportation costs. Instead, it is the control cost parameters b_i in K that give weight to the diagonal elements in Q. Andersson (1972) presents more exact conditions that have to hold if Q is to be positive semi-definite:

Theorem: The matrices G and K are assumed to be real and symmetric. Furthermore, K is assumed to be positive definite. A necessary and sufficient condition to make $G+K$, that is, Q, positive semi-definite is that all eigenvalues to $K^{-1}G$ are greater than, or equal to, -1.

The subsequent discussion, where the stability of the micro-units is investigated, assumes that Q is positive semi-definite. Whether the assumption is realistic or not is discussed later. Our way of treating optimum in the convex case follows the presentation of Snickars (1973, p.16).

The Lagrangean referring to (5.9), is:

$$L(x,u,v) = x \, Qx^T - u(f^T - Ex^T) + (\bar{x}^T - Ax^T)$$

where the variables u^h, $h = 1 \ldots H$ and v_i, $i = 1 \ldots n$ refer to constraints for available land and constraints for sector balances, respectively.

The dual corresponding to (5.9) is:

$$\max_{x, u, v} (\bar{x}\, v^T - f\, u^T - x\, Qx^T)$$

subject to

$$2\, Qx^T + (Eu)^T - (Av)^T \geqq 0$$

The dual variable u^h denotes the decrease in costs at a marginal increase of available land in h. v_i indicates the increase in value of the objective function at a marginal increase in production for sector i. u^h is therefore interpreted as a land rent in centre h and v_i as a semi-net revenue for sector i.

Assume that the solution implies a semi-net revenue $\hat{v}_i$ and the land rent $\hat{u}^h$ in centre h. If these are given, marginal profits for sector i situated in h are

$$\pi_i^h = \hat{v}_i - e_i \hat{u}^h - 2(Qx)_i^h$$

At optimum $\hat{x}$ all profits are non-positive, that is, $\hat{\pi}_i^h \leq 0$. For a move to be possible for a sector i from h to another centre, h', $x_i^h > 0$, that is $\hat{\pi}_i^h = 0$, must hold. The vector $\delta^T = (0, \ldots, -\delta, \ldots, \delta, \ldots 0)$ represents a move of δ output-units for sector i from h to h'. The effect of this on profits is:

$$\pi_i^{h'} - \hat{\pi}_i^h = \hat{v}_i - e_i \hat{u}^{h'} - 2(Q\hat{x})_i^{h'} - 2(Q\delta)_i^{h'}$$

There are no motives for a move if $\pi_i^{h'} - \hat{\pi}_i^h \geqq 0$. Since all profits are non-positive at optimum it is sufficient that $(Q\delta)_i^{h'} \geqq 0$ to prevent a relocation, that is:

$$(Q\delta)_i^{h'} = \left[b_i - (k_i + b_i^{h'h}) \right] \delta \geqq 0$$

If the micro-units are to have no incentives to move away from the locations indicated by optimum, an increase in output of a sector in another centre must imply the following: the increase of marginal control costs is greater than the decrease of marginal costs for the fixed capital, plus the decrease of marginal co-ordination costs. In other words: If optimum is to be maintained when decision-making is individual (and based on a system of semi-net revenues, v_i, and land rents, u^u) it is required that control costs are large in relation to economies of scale and co-ordination costs.[9]

Also in the non-convex case there is a global optimum that may be consistent with individual decision-making. Thus, even though the presentation above does not lead to the conclusion that individual decision-makers are in equilibrium at optimum, it is possible that a global optimum with no incentives for the micro-units to move out of optimum can be found on the basis of characteristics of Q other than that the matrix should be positive semi-definite. But if we extend the model and also discuss whether the dual variables can be used as price informers in a market process, we probably find that such a process leads to a local optimum in the non-convex case. The convex case is therefore more interesting.

If (5.9) is to be convex, the conditions of the previous theorem should hold. The question is then whether these are realistic. In the first place, it is improbable that G is symmetric. This is due to the input-output coefficients. International comparisons of input-output tables show that these have a common structure that is not symmetric. Instead, one-way dependencies are usual. Simpson and Tsukui (1965) show that the structure is nearly triangular (in a triangular matrix, sectors are so ordered that all elements on one side of the diagonal are zero). Lamel, Richter, and Teufelbauer (1972) have obtained similar results, but they also show that mutual dependencies are greater, the more economically developed a country is.

K, however, is symmetric. Convexity furthermore requires that the matrix be positive definite. Simplifying, this implies that the same condition that guarantees stability for the micro-units must hold, namely, that control costs should be great in relation to co-ordination costs. If the eigenvalue condition is to be fulfilled, the valuation of transportation costs and costs for the fixed capital should be small in relation to the valuation of those inputs whose employment is influenced by control and co-ordination systems.[10]

The conclusion is that we cannot be sure whether the conditions for convexity are realistic. Thus, the question whether stability for the micro-units holds cannot be given anything but a tentative answer. This is primarily an empirical problem that has not yet been fully studied. Thus chapter 5 is more preliminary than the previous chapters.

No calculations have been undertaken on the basis of (5.9). It is therefore impossible to say if optimum agrees with the structure of the systems of centres discussed in chapter 2. The assumptions concerning the transportation cost function entail, however, that the transportation flows can never be like those of Christaller or Tinbergen. As long as a selling sector has any plant situated in centres of lower rank than a plant of a buying sector, there are always deliveries going from centres of lower rank to centres of higher rank. The solution should therefore be regarded as an approximation. It is thus possible to adjust optimum by replacing opposite flows of the same commodity between centres with one flow, without thereby affecting the availability of a product in a centre. This flow is determined as the difference between the commodity flows and takes the same direction as the dominating flow. The result is a new solution where transportation costs are lower than at optimum of (5.9). After such an adjustment, the model can, among other things, be used for testing the realism of Tinbergen's hypothesis.

NOTES

1. The following equation is stipulated: $AC(c) = AP(c) + AT(c)$ where
   AC(c) total average costs
   AP(c) average production costs
   AT(c) average transportation costs

   c plant capacity

   AC(c) has a minimum when the following conditions are fulfilled:

   $AT_c = -AP_c$ and $AT_{cc} > AP_{cc}$
2. All transformations are assumed to be linear, or possible to make linear.
3. This question ('The metering problem') is discussed by Alchian and Demsetz (1972).
4. With our assumption it would be more correct to write $R(y)$.
5. When determining fixed costs, factor prices are assumed given. It is probable that these prices are influenced by transportation costs, and thus by the structure of the system of centres. There are thus objections to level against our way of treating fixed costs.
6. The assumption implies a certain overrating of the importance of economies of scale.
7. It is assumed that each plant corresponds to one agent.
8. Inputs corresponding to the different types of costs in the objective function are not taken from the given total outputs of the sectors, but are assumed to be added outside

the model. This implies that the part of co-ordination costs which concerns inefficient combinations of factors does not influence the value of the input-output coefficients in the model.

9. There is a relationship between commodity prices, p_j, and semi-net revenues, v_i, namely $v_i = p_i \sum j \, v_{ii} p_i i, j = 1 \ldots n$. Since v_i, $i = 1 \ldots n$, is determined by the optimal program, it is thus possible to determine a corresponding price system.

10. Åke E. Andersson (1972) has based his reasoning on the following relationship between Q, G and K: $Q = \alpha G + (1 - \alpha)K$, where G is a communication cost matrix, K a congestion cost matrix, and α the relative value attributed by a household or an enterprise to accessibility in relation to congestion. Theorem 2 then implies that the eigenvalues for $K^{-1} G$ must not fall below $-1 - \alpha/\alpha$. Only when the valuation of accessibility is sufficiently reduced can the condition be met. If production and transportation costs are measured in units of capital, and control and co-ordination costs in working hours, matrices can be weighted also in our case. α then denotes the relative valuation of a capital unit in relation to a working hour. If α is made sufficiently small the condition is also met in our case.

Appendix 1

Municipal blocks composing the three metropolitan areas:

Stockholm metropolitan area		Malmö metropolitan area	
0101	Stockholm	1206	Kävlinge
0105	Sigtuna	1207	Lund
0106	Vallentuna	1208	Lomma
0108	Vaxholm	1209	Malmö
0109	Upplands-Väsby	1210	Vellinge
0110	Järfälla	1211	Trelleborg
0111	Sollentuna		
0112	Solna/Sundbyberg	Gothenburg metropolitan area	
0113	Ekerö	1305	Kungsbacka
0114	Täby	1401	Härryda
0115	Danderyd	1402	Partille
0116	Lidingö	1403	Mölndal
0117	Gustavsberg	1404	Gothenburg
0118	Nacka	1405	Öckerö
0119	Tyresö	1406	Kungälv
0120	Haninge	1407	Stenungsund
0121	Huddinge	1408	Tjörn
0122	Botkyrka	1508	Surte
0123	Nynäshamn	1509	Lerum
0124	Södertälje		
0126	Upplands-Bro		

Ranking of municipal blocks:

Rank	Municipal block		Rank	Municipal block	
1	—	Stockholm	13	2101	Gävle
2	—	Gothenburg	14	2202	Sundsvall
3	—	Malmö	15	1704	Karlstad
4	1901	Västerås	16	1301	Halmstad
5	0303	Uppsala	17	2401	Umeå
6	0510	Norrköping	18	1506	Trollhättan
7	1801	Örebro	19	0705	Växjö
8	1202	Helsingborg	20	1808	Karlskoga
9	0601	Jönköping	21	2505	Luleå
10	0508	Linköping	22	1001	Karlskrona
11	1517	Borås	23	2002	Borlänge
12	0405	Eskilstuna	24	1410	Uddevalla

Rank	Municipal block		Rank	Municipal block	
25	0809	Kalmar	71	1712	Arvika
26	1103	Kristianstad	72	1902	Hallstahammar
27	0401	Nyköping	73	2106	Bollnäs
28	1204	Landskrona	74	0502	Mjölby
29	2209	Örnsköldsvik	75	1516	Mark (Kinna)
30	0501	Motala	76	0103	Norrtälje
31	1613	Skövde	77	0701	Ljungby
32	2001	Falun	78	0807	Nybro
33	2102	Sandviken	79	1906	Arboga
34	2406	Skellefteå	80	0606	Vetlanda
35	2303	Östersund	81	1201	Höganäs
36	1505	Vänersborg	82	1709	Säffle
37	2514	Kiruna	83	2103	Hofors
38	0403	Katrineholm	84	2204	Timrå
39	1904	Köping	85	1606	Skara
40	1604	Lidköping	86	1005	Olofström
41	1701	Kristinehamn	87	1910	Sala
42	2006	Avesta	88	0406	Strängnäs
43	0801	Västervik	89	1004	Sölvesborg
44	2007	Ludvika	90	1705	Hammarö
45	0604	Nässjö	91	1501	Åmål
46	0302	Enköping	92	0605	Eksjö
47	1510	Alingsäs	93	1807	Degerfors
48	2205	Härnösand	94	1717	Hagfors
49	2506	Boden	95	1111	Åstrop
50	0901	Gotland Visby	96	2206	Kramfors
51	1002	Ronneby	97	2207	Sollefteå
52	1003	Karlshamn	98	1203	Bjuv
53	1304	Varberg	99	1109	Klippan
54	2501	Piteå	100	2013	Mora
55	1107	Hässleholm	101	0507	Åtvidaberg
56	0805	Oskarshamn	102	1609	Tidah
57	0509	Finspång	103	2008	Smedjebacken
58	1615	Mariestad	104	1513	Ulricehamn
59	0609	Värnamo	105	0704	Alvesta
60	1607	Falköping	106	1811	Lindesberg
61	1112	Ängelholm	107	1810	Hällefors
62	1907	Fagersta	108	0611	Gislaved
63	0602	Tranås	109	1611	Tibro
64	1303	Falkenberg	110	2005	Hedemora
65	1213	Ystad	111	1104	Bromölla
66	2109	Hudiksvall	112	2408	Lycksele
67	1215	Eslöv	113	1703	Filipstad
68	0402	Oxelösund	114	1411	Lysekil
69	2105	Söderhamn	115	0407	Flen
70	1802	Kumla	116	0802	Vimmerby

Rank	Municipal block		Rank	Municipal block	
117	2108	Ljusdal	163	2510	Haparanda
118	2513	Gällivare	164	1409	Orust
119	1708	Grums	165	1511	Vårgårda
120	2508	Kalix	166	1612	Karlsborg
121	0703	Älmhult	167	1812	Ljusnasberg
122	1102	Tomelilla	168	1205	Svalöv
123	1108	Perstorp	169	1502	Bengtsfors
124	1106	Osby	170	2502	Älvsbyn
125	1903	Surahammar	171	0506	Kisa
126	1101	Simrishamn	172	0504	Boxholm
127	1809	Nora	173	2201	Ånge
128	1905	Kungsör	174	2305	Strömsund
129	0404	Vingåker	175	1512	Herrljunga
130	1216	Hörby	176	1413	Munkedal
131	1302	Laholm	177	1504	Mellerud
132	0806	Mönsterås	178	1702	Storfors
133	1212	Skurup	179	1105	Broby
134	1217	Höör	180	0512	Valdemarsvik
135	1806	Laxå	181	0608	Vaggeryd
136	2010	Malung	182	1412	Gravarne
137	1507	Lilla Edet	183	1414	Tanum
138	2107	Ovanåker	184	2411	Vilhelmina
139	1415	Strömstad	185	2104	Ockelbo
140	1706	Kil	186	0612	Hyltebruk
141	0808	Emmaboda	187	2503	Arvidsjaur
142	2011	Leksand	188	0308	Östhammar
143	2404	Vännäs	189	1514	Tranemo
144	2014	Orsa	190	1608	Habo
145	0702	Markaryd	191	1805	Askersund
146	0803	Hultsfred	192	0610	Gnosjö
147	1909	Norberg	193	1113	Båstad
148	1714	Torsby	194	1515	Svenljunga
149	0511	Söderköping	195	2015	Älvdalen
150	0607	Sävsjö	196	2402	Nordmaling
151	1605	Götene	197	0503	Ödeshög
152	1718	Munkfors	198	1601	Grästorp
153	0306	Tierp	199	1616	Gullspång
154	1614	Töreboda	200	2409	Storuman
155	1707	Forshaga	201	2507	Jokkmokk
156	1713	Sunne	202	0603	Aneby
157	2004	Säter	203	0706	Tingsryd
158	1603	Vara	204	0708	Lessebo
159	1214	Sjöbo	205	1503	Färgelanda
160	2012	Rättvik	206	1908	Skinnskatteberg
161	1110	Örkelljunga	207	1911	Heby
162	1610	Hjo	208	0812	Borgholm

Rank	Municipal block		Rank	Municipal block	
209	0707	Uppvidinge	224	0811	Mörbylånga
210	2009	Vansbro	225	2003	Gagnef
211	2309	Sveg	226	2407	Norsjö
212	0810	Torsås	227	2509	Överkalix
213	1710	Årjäng	228	0307	Älvkarleby
214	1711	Eda	229	2307	Järpen
215	1716	Kyrkheden	230	2512	Pajala
216	2412	Åsele	231	2504	Arjeplog
217	0804	Högsby	232	2405	Robertsfors
218	2302	Bräcke	233	2410	Storsele
219	2306	Krokom	234	2308	Berg
220	2511	Övertorneå	235	2301	Hammarstrand
221	2403	Vindeln	236	0505	Ydre
222	1803	Hallsberg	237	1715	Finnskoga/Dalby
223	2110	Bergsjö			

Appendix 2

Municipal blocks clustered according to component values
Components 1–10

COMPONENT 1

Rank of municipal block	Component value	Rank of municipal block	Component value
5	0,115	30	0,110
7	0,134	38	0,079
10	0,119	40	0,101
11	0,128	41	0,077
12	0,110	43	0,104
15	0,108	49	0,455
16	0,130	64	0,108
18	0,073	70	0,062
19	0,117	77	0,097
22	0,106	149	0,015
25	0,108	157	0,024
26	0,117	159	0,031
28	0,075	164	0,020

COMPONENT 2

Rank of municipal block	Component value	Rank of municipal block	Component value
1	0,417	82	−0,094
2	0,374	83	−0,058
3	0,381	86	−0,058
6	0,173	93	−0,050
8	0,194	101	−0,072
9	0,144	105	−0,079
		110	−0,101
		112	−0,079
		117	−0,094
		119	−0,050
		130	−0,058
		138	−0,079
		141	−0,137

Component 2 (*continued*)

Rank of municipal block	Component value	Rank of municipal block	Component value
		148	−0,050
		153	−0,101
		163	−0,058
		166	−0,022
		170	−0,058
		171	−0,065
		172	−0,050
		174	−0,079
		178	−0,014
		180	−0,065
		185	−0,036
		187	−0,065

COMPONENT 3

Rank of municipal block	Component value	Rank of municipal block	Component value
13	0,215	46	−0,084
14	0,243	47	−0,103
17	0,150	53	−0,121
20	0,075	55	−0,121
21	0,178	57	−0,103
23	0,121	59	−0,187
24	0,121	75	−0,112
29	0,103	80	−0,103
32	0,112	102	−0,103
34	0,168	104	−0,121
35	0,140	108	−0,206
36	0,131	123	−0,056
37	0,103	124	−0,112
44	0,131	145	−0,084
48	0,093	146	−0,093
50	0,150	152	−0,028
56	0,103	154	−0,065
62	0,075	189	−0,168
66	0,121		
68	0,047		
90	0,028		
94	0,056		
111	0,065		
118	0,093		

Component 3 (*continued*)

Rank of municipal block	Component value	Rank of municipal block	Component value
137	0,037		
140	0,084		
143	0,075		
168	0,047		
173	0,056		
184	0,037		

COMPONENT 4

Rank of municipal block	Component value	Rank of municipal block	Component value
63	0,144	33	−0,144
161	0,111	42	−0,122
		84	−0,100
		88	−0,122
		107	−0,100
		120	−0,133
		125	−0,100
		127	−0,122
		135	−0,156
		147	−0,100
		155	−0,100
		162	−0,100
		167	−0,122
		186	−0,133
		188	−0,122

COMPONENT 5

Rank of municipal block	Component value	Rank of municipal block	Component value
27	0,188	58	−0,129
39	0,129	60	−0,129
65	0,165	73	−0,106
67	0,141	78	−0,106
74	0,129	116	−0,118
76	0,153	175	−0,141
85	0,118	177	−0,165
113	0,165		
144	0,106		
181	0,106		

COMPONENT 6

Rank of municipal block	Component value	Rank of municipal block	Component value
45	0,108	51	−0,108
106	0,157	52	−0,108
		121	−0,181
		129	−0,108
		142	−0,169
		182	−0,133

COMPONENT 7

Rank of municipal block	Component value	Rank of municipal block	Component value
4	0,207	31	−0,146
79	0,110	61	−0,110
128	0,134	71	−0,110
		99	−0,134
		134	−0,110
		160	−0,122
		179	−0,110

COMPONENT 8

Rank of municipal block	Component value	Rank of municipal block	Component value
95	0,125	109	−0,100
158	0,100	122	−0,100
165	0,188	136	−0,138
190	0,150	151	−0,150
		156	−0,138
		169	−0,125
		183	−0,100

COMPONENT 9

Rank of municipal block	Component value	Rank of municipal block	Component value
72	0,167	54	−0,167
100	0,141	69	−0,103
103	0,103	89	−0,205
131	0,103	91	−0,128
		92	−0,103
		115	−0,115
		126	−0,192
		132	−0,103
		133	−0,115

COMPONENT 10

Rank of municipal block	Component value	Rank of municipal block	Component value
87	0,120	81	−0,120
176	0,133	96	−0,133
		97	−0,120
		98	−0,107
		114	−0,120
		139	−0,147
		150	−0,147

Appendix 3

Sectors clustered according to factor loadings. Components 1–10.

GROUP a (COMPONENT 1)

SNI	Denomination	Factor loading	Number of establish-ments
31121	Manufacture of dairy products	0,185	173
31179	Manufacture of bakery products	0,209	604
32150	Cordage, rope and twine industries	0,015	13
34201	Printing and newspaper publishing	0,236	749
35512	Rubber industry – repairing, rebuilding and retreading	0,117	92
35609	Manufacture of plastic products	0,143	225
36919	Manufacture of bricks	0,013	10
36991	Manufacture of stone products	0,134	159
36992	Manufacture of concrete and concrete products	0,236	475
38130	Manufacture of structural metal products	0,233	683
38199	Manufacture of metal products	0,214	670
38249	Manufacture of special industrial machinery and equipment, except metal and wood working machinery	0,165	265
38299	Manufacture of machinery and equipment not elsewhere classified	0,183	410
38432	Manufacture of motor engines, spare parts and trailers	0,178	247
39030	Manufacture of sporting and athletic goods	0,031	26

GROUP b (COMPONENT 3)

SNI	Denomination	Factor loading	Number of establish-ments
32130	Knitting mills	0,121	156
32204	Manufacture of wearing apparel – outerwear	0,196	330

Group b (Component 3) (*continued*)

SNI	Denomination	Factor loading	Number of establish-ments
32206	Sewing industry	0,140	152
32310	Tanneries and leather finishing	0,019	10
32400	Manufacture of footwear, except vulcanized or moulded rubber or plastic footwear	0,121	122
33190	Manufacture of wood and cork products not elsewhere classified	0,271	192
33201	Manufacture of upholstered furniture except primarily of metal	0,234	106
33202	Manufacture of unholstered furniture except primarily of metal	0,374	333
33209	Manufacture of wooden furniture, not elsewhere classified, except primarily of metal	0,075	29
35511	Tyre and tube industries	0,028	9
36203	Manufacture of table and ornamental glass	0,037	37
38110	Manufacture of cutlery, hand tools and general hardware	0,159	150
38120	Manufacture of furniture and fixtures primarily of metal	0,178	82
38193	Manufacture of nails, screws and bolts	0,093	62
38194	Manufacture of structural metal products not elsewhere classified	0,159	136

GROUP c (COMPONENT 3)

SNI	Denomination	Factor loading	Number of establish-ments
31111	Slaughtering	−0,140	72
31112	Preparing and preserving meat	−0,224	192
31330	Malt liquors and malt	−0,140	77
31340	Soft drinks and carbonated waters industries	−0,103	74
32203	Manufacture of fur wearing apparel	−0,131	71
34111	Manufacture of pulp	−0,103	47

Group c (Component 3) (*continued*)

SNI	Denomination	Factor loading	Number of establish-ments
34112	Manufacture of paper and paper-board	− 0,103	64
34113	Manufacture of fibreboard	− 0,056	12
35112	Manufacture of organic chemicals	− 0,093	29
35113	Manufacture of oxygen and other industrial gas	− 0,121	41
35121	Manufacture of fertilizers	− 0,047	8
37102	Ferro-alloying industry	− 0,019	3
37201	Manufacture of primary non-ferrous metal products from ore	− 0,037	3
38241	Manufacture of machinery for processing pulp and paper	− 0,076	29
38292	Repair shops for machinery and equipment except household apparatus	− 0,168	249
38310	Manufacture of electrical industrial machinery and apparatus	− 0,131	63
38320	Manufacture of radio, television and communication equipment and apparatus	− 0,131	99
38394	Repair shops for electrical products except household apparatus	− 0,168	123
38421	Manufacture of railroad equipment	− 0,056	7
38422	Repair of railroad equipment	− 0,178	57
38452	Repair of aircraft	− 0,084	25

GROUP d (COMPONENT 2)

SNI	Denomination	Factor loading	Number of establish-ments
31151	Production of margarine	− 0,072	4
31159	Manufacture of vegetable and animal oils and fats	− 0,058	4
31160	Grain mill products	− 0,108	28
31171	Manufacture of crispbread	− 0,036	11
31180	Sugar factories and refineries	− 0,043	8

Group d (Component 2) (*continued*)

SNI	Denomination	Factor loading	Number of establish-ments
31190	Manufacture of cocoa, chocolate and sugar confectionery	−0,108	49
31212	Coffee roasting	−0,115	18
31219	Manufacture of food products	−0,122	37
31220	Manufacture of prepared animal feeds	−0,115	39
31312	Manufacture of alcoholic liquors	−0,086	8
31400	Tobacco manufactures	−0,072	4
32112	Weaving textiles	−0,108	88
32120	Manufacture of made-up textile goods except wearing apparel	−0,108	122
32190	Manufacture of textiles not elsewhere classified	−0,086	31
32201	Manufacture of hats and caps	−0,108	44
32320	Fur dressing and dyeing industries	−0,014	4
34121	Manufacture of corrugated paperboard	−0,086	15
37204	Foundries for nonferrous metal	−0,108	66
38191	Manufacture of metal containers	−0,043	29
38192	Manufacture of metal wires, netting, wire cables, wire ropes	−0,079	50
38210	Manufacture of engines and turbines	−0,029	5
38251	Manufacture of computing machinery	−0,043	6
38391	Manufacture of insulated wires and cables	−0,079	12
38392	Manufacture of storage and primary batteries	−0,079	13
38393	Manufacture of electrical light bulbs and fluorescent tubes	−0,108	21
38413	Manufacture of ship and boat engines	−0,043	5
38431	Manufacture of motor vehicles	−0,079	14
38451	Manufacture of aircraft	−0,072	9
38510	Manufacture of professional and scientific, measuring and controlling equipment not elsewhere classified	−0,115	111
38520	Manufacture of photographic and optical goods	−0,108	20
39010	Manufacture of jewellery and related articles	−0,086	43
39020	Manufacture of musical instruments	−0,036	18
39090	Manufacturing industries not elsewhere classified	−0,129	84

Group d (Component 2) *(continued)*

SNI	Denomination	Factor loading	Number of establish- ments
34129	Manufacture of containers and boxes of paper and paperboard not else- where classified	−0,151	81
34190	Manufacture of pulp, paper and paper- board articles not elsewhere classified	−0,115	50
34202	Manufacture of type foundries	−0,173	109
34203	Bookbinding	−0,122	94
35111	Manufacture of basic industrial in- organic chemicals	−0,108	24
35122	Manufacture of herbicides and insecti- cides	−0,058	3
35131	Manufacture of plastic materials and man-made fibres	−0,115	16
35210	Manufacture of paints, varnishes and lacquers	−0,108	48
35220	Manufacture of drugs and medicines	−0,122	22
35230	Manufacture of soap and cleaning preparations, perfumes, cosmetics and other toilet preparations	−0,101	45
35300	Petroleum refineries	−0,086	5
35401	Manufacture of lubricating oils and greases	−0,094	12
35409	Manufacture of products of petroleum and coal not elsewhere classified	−0,122	23
35590	Manufacture of rubber products not elsewhere classified	−0,115	60
36100	Manufacture of pottery, china and earthenware	−0,065	24
36202	Manufacture of container glass	−0,029	3
36209	Manufacture of glass products not elsewhere classified	−0,079	25
36921	Manufacture of cement	−0,050	7
36922	Manufacture of lime	−0,050	21
37202	Industry for extracting non-ferrous metals from scrap-iron	−0,050	8
37203	Rolling mills, drawing mills etc for non-ferrous metals	−0,058	14

GROUP e (COMPONENT 2)

SNI	Denomination	Factor loading
31211	Manufacture of starch	0,014
33111	Sawmills, planing mills and industry for the preservation of wood	0,281
33112	Manufacture of wooden houses and wooden building materials	0,252

GROUP f (COMPONENT 4)

SNI	Denomination	Factor loading
37101	Iron and steel works	−0,289

GROUP g (COMPONENT 5)

SNI	Denomination	Factor loading
38220	Manufacture of agricultural machinery and equipment	0,188

GROUP h (COMPONENT 5)

SNI	Denomination	Factor loading
38259	Manufacture of office machinery not elsewhere classified	−0,118

GROUP i (COMPONENT 6)

SNI	Denomination	Factor loading
32209	Manufacture of wearing apparel not elsewhere classified	0,157

GROUP j (COMPONENT 6)

SNI	Denomination	Factor loading
32330	Manufacture of products of leather and leather substitutes except footwear and wearing apparel	−0,145
33119	Manufacture of wood materials not elsewhere classified	−0,108
37103	Iron and steel foundries	−0,241
38232	Manufacture of wood-working machinery	−0,169

GROUP k (COMPONENT 7)

SNI	Denomination	Factor loading
32111	Manufacture of yarn	0,244
33120	Manufacture of wooden and cane containers and small cane ware	0,293
35290	Manufacture of chemical products not elsewhere classified	0,134
36911	Manufacture of architectural terracotta	0,171
38490	Manufacture of transport equipment not elsewhere classified	0,171

GROUP l (COMPONENT 7)

SNI	Denomination	Factor loading
38195	Manufacture of household metal products	−0,232
38399	Manufacture of electrical apparatus and supplies not elsewhere classified	−0,268
38412	Building and repair of boats	−0,244

GROUP m (COMPONENT 8)

SNI	Denomination	Factor loading
32202	Manufacture of leather wearing apparel	0,125
38330	Manufacture of electrical appliances and houseware	0,175

GROUP n (COMPONENT 8)

SNI	Denomination	Factor loading
32113	Bleaching, dyeing and other industries engaged in preparing textiles	−0,100
32140	Manufacture of carpets and rugs	−0,100
32205	Manufacture of shirts and underwear	−0,100
35601	Manufacture of plastic containers	−0,150

GROUP o (COMPONENT 9)

SNI	Denomination	Factor loading
31122	Manufacture of ice cream	−0,103
31130	Canning and preserving of fruits and vegetables	−0,128
31140	Canning, preserving and processing of fish, crustacea and similar foods	−0,128
31311	Destilling alcoholic liquors from potatoes	−0,103
38291	Manufacture of household apparatus	−0,115

GROUP p (COMPONENT 10)

SNI	Denomination	Factor loading
38242	Manufacture of machinery and equipment for construction and mining industries	0,347

GROUP q (COMPONENT 10)

SNI	Denomination	Factor loading
35132	Manufacture of plastic products	−0,147
36999	Manufacture of mineral products not elsewhere classified	−0,107
38411	Shipyards	−0,133
38440	Manufacture of motorcycles and bicycles	−0,133

Appendix 4

Detailed presentation of the result of the calculations in 4:4

The first assumption with the small coefficient relating final demand for agricultural production to income.

PRODUCTION WITHIN EACH SECTOR AND CENTRE

Centre	0.	Sector 00.	1.	2.	3.	4.	Sum
A	121	0	6088	2500	2372	2877	13 958
B	121	0	196	113	0	0	430
C	121	109	331	142	0	0	703
D	121	109	331	142	0	0	703
E	121	0	196	113	0	0	430
F	121	0	647	225	462	0	1 455
G	121	0	647	225	462	0	1 455
Sum	847	218	8436	3460	3296	2877	19 134
Cap	0	0	0	113	446	2152	

EXPORTS AND IMPORTS[1]

Centre A	0.	00.	1.	2.	3.	4.
A	0	0	0	0	0	0
B	−110	0	0	0	0	60
C	−105	−91	0	0	0	95
D	−105	−84	0	0	0	95
E	−110	0	0	0	0	60
F	−38	0	0	0	0	185
G	−38	0	0	0	0	185

Centre B						
A	110	0	0	0	0	−60
B	0	0	0	0	0	0
C	0	0	0	0	0	0
D	0	−3	0	0	0	0
E	0	0	0	0	0	0
F	0	0	0	22	−68	0
G	0	0	0	0	0	0

1. Positive values for experts and negative for imports.

Centre C	0.	00.	1.	2.	3.	4.
A	105	91	0	0	0	−95
B	0	0	0	0	0	0
C	0	0	0	0	0	0
D	0	0	0	0	0	0
E	0	0	0	0	0	0
F	0	0	0	0	0	0
G	0	0	0	0	−109	0

Centre D						
A	105	84	0	0	0	−95
B	0	3	0	0	0	0
C	0	0	0	0	0	0
D	0	0	0	0	0	0
E	0	3	0	0	0	0
F	0	9	0	0	−109	0
G	0	0	0	0	0	0

Centre E						
A	110	0	0	0	0	−60
B	0	0	0	0	0	0
C	0	0	0	0	0	0
D	0	−3	0	0	0	0
E	0	0	0	0	0	0
F	0	0	0	0	0	0
G	0	0	0	22	−68	0

Centre F						
A	38	0	0	0	0	−185
B	0	0	0	−22	68	0
C	0	0	0	0	0	0
D	0	−9	0	0	109	0
E	0	0	0	0	0	0
F	0	0	0	0	0	0
G	0	0	0	0	0	0

Centre G	0.	00.	1.	2.	3.	4.
A	38	0	0	0	0	−185
B	0	0	0	0	0	0
C	0	−8	0	0	109	0
D	0	0	0	0	0	0
E	0	0	0	−22	68	0
F	0	0	0	0	0	0
G	0	0	0	0	0	0

The second assumption with the small coefficient relating final demand for agricultural production to income.

PRODUCTION WITHIN EACH SECTOR AND CENTRE

Centre	0.	Sector 00.	1.	2.	3.	4.	Sum
A	121	0	6183	2590	2407	2877	14 178
B	121	0	112	0	0	0	233
C	121	109	331	142	0	0	703
D	121	109	331	142	0	0	703
E	121	0	112	0	0	0	233
F	121	0	684	293	445	0	1 543
G	121	0	684	293	445	0	1 543
Sum	847	218	8437	3460	3297	2877	19 136
Cap	0	0	0	113	446	2152	

EXPORTS AND IMPORTS

Centre A

A	0	0	0	0	0	0
B	−113	0	0	19	0	35
C	−105	−88	0	0	0	95
D	−105	−88	0	0	0	95
E	−113	0	0	19	0	35
F	−38	0	0	0	0	197
G	−38	0	0	0	0	197

Centre B	0.	00.	1.	2.	3.	4.
A	113	0	0	−19	0	−35
B	0	0	0	0	0	0
C	0	−1	0	0	0	0
D	0	0	0	0	0	0
E	0	0	0	0	0	0
F	0	0	0	−16	−43	0
G	0	0	0	0	0	0

Centre C						
A	105	88	0	0	0	−95
B	0	1	0	0	0	0
C	0	0	0	0	0	0
D	0	0	0	0	0	0
E	0	1	0	0	0	0
F	0	0	0	0	0	0
G	0	9	0	0	−109	0

Centre D						
A	105	89	0	0	0	−95
B	0	0	0	0	0	0
C	0	0	0	0	0	0
D	0	0	0	0	0	0
E	0	0	0	0	0	0
F	0	9	0	0	−109	0
G	0	0	0	0	0	0

Centre E						
A	113	0	0	−19	0	−35
B	0	0	0	0	0	0
C	0	−1	0	0	0	0
D	0	0	0	0	0	0
E	0	0	0	0	0	0
F	0	0	0	0	0	0
G	0	0	0	−16	−43	0

Centre F	0.	00.	1.	2.	3.	4.
A	38	0	0	0	0	−197
B	0	0	0	16	43	0
C	0	0	0	0	0	0
D	0	−9	0	0	109	0
E	0	0	0	0	0	0
F	0	0	0	0	0	0
G	0	0	0	0	0	0

Centre G						
A	38	0	0	0	0	−197
B	0	0	0	0	0	0
C	0	−9	0	0	109	0
D	0	0	0	0	0	0
E	0	0	0	16	43	0
F	0	0	0	0	0	0
G	0	0	0	0	0	0

The first assumption with the large coefficient relating final demand for agricultural production to income.

PRODUCTION WITHIN EACH SECTOR AND CENTRE

Centre	0.	Sector 00.	1.	2.	3.	4.	Sum
A	239	0	5118	1427	2028	2865	11 677
B	239	0	283	82	0	0	604
C	239	98	415	123	0	0	875
D	239	98	415	123	0	0	875
E	239	0	283	82	0	0	604
F	239	0	932	247	662	0	2 080
G	239	0	932	247	662	0	2 080
Sum	1673	196	8378	2331	3352	2865	18 795
Cap	0	0	0	76	445	2152	

EXPORTS AND IMPORTS

Centre A	0.	00.	1.	2.	3.	4.
A	0	0	0	0	0	0
B	−194	0	0	0	0	87
C	−177	−75	0	0	0	122
D	−177	−75	0	0	0	122
E	−194	0	0	0	0	87
F	−30	0	0	0	0	268
G	−30	0	0	0	0	268

Centre B						
A	194	0	0	0	0	−87
B	0	0	0	0	0	0
C	0	0	0	0	0	0
D	0	0	0	0	0	0
E	0	0	0	0	0	0
F	0	−3	0	0	−104	0
G	0	0	0	0	0	0

Centre C						
A	177	75	0	0	0	−122
B	0	0	0	0	0	0
C	0	0	0	0	0	0
D	0	0	0	0	0	0
E	0	3	0	0	0	0
F	0	0	0	0	0	0
G	0	9	0	0	−143	0

Centre D						
A	177	75	0	0	0	−122
B	0	3	0	0	0	0
C	0	0	0	0	0	0
D	0	0	0	0	0	0
E	0	0	0	0	0	0
F	0	10	0	0	−143	0
G	0	0	0	0	0	0

Centre E	0.	00.	1.	2.	3.	4.
A	194	0	0	0	0	−87
B	0	0	0	0	0	0
C	0	−3	0	0	0	0
D	0	0	0	0	0	0
E	0	0	0	0	0	0
F	0	0	0	0	0	0
G	0	0	0	0	−104	0

Centre F						
A	30	0	0	0	0	−268
B	0	0	0	0	104	0
C	0	0	0	0	0	0
D	0	−10	0	0	143	0
E	0	0	0	0	0	0
F	0	0	0	0	0	0
G	0	0	0	0	0	0

Centre G						
A	30	0	0			−268
B	0	0	0	0	0	0
C	0	−9	0	0	143	0
D	0	0	0	0	0	0
E	0	0	0	0	104	0
F	0	0	0	0	0	0
G	0	0	0	0	0	0

Special regions for agriculture and extractive industry, respectively (OPHELIE).

PRODUCTION WITHIN EACH SECTOR AND CENTRE

Centre	0.	Sector 00.	1.	2.	3.	4.	Sum
A	0	0	84	113	0	0	197
B	281	0	902	387	445	0	2 015
C	0	73	75	0	0	0	148
D	281	0	878	354	445	0	1 958
E	0	73	75	0	0	0	148
F	281	0	6345	2607	2407	2877	14 517
G	0	73	75	0	0	0	148
Sum	843	219	8434	3461	3297	2877	19 131
Cap	0	0	0	113	446	2152	

EXPORTS AND IMPORTS

Centre A	0.	00.	1.	2.	3.	4.
A	0	0	0	0	0	0
B	−3	0	0	0	−25	0
C	0	0	0	8	0	0
D	0	0	0	0	0	0
E	0	0	0	24	0	0
F	0	0	0	0	0	−25
G	0	−2	0	24	0	0

Centre B						
A	3	0	0	0	25	0
B	0	0	0	0	0	0
C	3	−12	0	16	23	0
D	0	0	0	0	0	0
E	0	0	0	0	0	0
F	178	0	0	0	3	−264
G	3	0	0	0	23	0

Centre C						
A	0	0	0	−8	0	0
B	−3	12	0	−16	−23	0
C	0	0	0	0	0	0
D	0	0	0	0	0	0
E	0	0	0	0	0	0
F	0	56	0	0	0	−19
G	0	0	0	0	0	0

Centre D						
A	0	0	0	0	0	0
B	0	0	0	0	0	0
C	0	0	0	0	0	0
D	0	0	0	0	0	0
E	3	−11	0	0	23	0
F	185	0	0	0	58	−257
G	0	0	0	0	0	0

Centre E	0.	00.	1.	2.	3.	4.
A	0	0	0	−24	0	0
B	0	0	0	0	0	0
C	0	0	0	0	0	0
D	−3	11	0	0	−23	0
E	0	0	0	0	0	0
F	0	57	0	0	0	−19
G	0	0	0	0	0	0

Centre F						
A	0	0	0	0	0	25
B	−178	0	0	0	−3	264
C	0	−56	0	0	0	19
D	−185	0	0	0	−58	257
E	0	−57	0	0	0	19
F	0	0	0	0	0	0
G	0	−66	0	0	0	19

Centre G						
A	0	2	0	−24	0	0
B	−3	0	0	0	−23	0
C	0	0	0	0	0	0
D	0	0	0	0	0	0
E	0	0	0	0	0	0
F	0	66	0	0	0	−19
G	0	0	0	0	0	0

References

Abadie, J. (ed.), *Integer and nonlinear programming*, Amsterdam 1970.

Agin, N., Optimum seeking with Branch and Bound, *Management Science*, vol. 13, pp. B 176–185, New York 1966.

Alchian, A. A. and H. Demsetz, Production, information costs and economic organization, *American Economic Review*, vol. 62, no 5, pp. 777–795, Wisconsin 1972.

Allen, G. R., The 'Courbe des Populations' a further analysis, *Bulletin of the Oxford University Institute of Statistics*, vol. 16, pp. 179–189, Oxford 1954.

Amin, S., *L'accumulation à l'échelle mondiale*, Paris 1970.

Anderson, Å. E. and R. Jungen, *Storstadsproblematiken*, (Problems of metropolitan areas) Stockholm 1970.

Andersson, Å. E., *On the problem of optimal congestion*, Department of Economics, University of Gothenburg 1972 (stencil).

Andersson, Å, E, and B. Marksjö General equilibrium models for allocation in space under interdependency and increasing returns to scale, *Regional and urban Economics*, vol. 2, no 2, pp. 133–158, Amsterdam 1972.

Andersson, Å. E., Revidera regionalpolitiken, (Revise the Regional Policy), *Ekonomisk Debatt*, no 2, Stockholm 1973.

Andersson, Å. E. and B. Marksjö, Konfliktanalys (Conflict Analysis), *Nordiska institutet för samhällsplanering*, Stockholm. (stencil)

Artle, R., Stor-Stockholms ekonomiska struktur (The Structure of the Stockholm Economy), *FFI-meddelande nr 54, del II* 1957.

Bain, J. S., *International differences in industrial structure. Eight nations in the 1950 s*, New Haven & London 1966.

Balas, E., Discrete Programming by the filter method, *Operation Research*, vol. 15, pp. 915–957, Baltimore 1967.

Baligh, H. H. and L. E. Richartz, An analysis of vertical market structures, *Management Science*, vol. 10, no 4, pp. 667–689, New York 1964.

Baumol, W. J., *Economic theory and operational analysis*, Prentice-Hall 1965.

Beale, E. M. Survey of integer programming. *Operational Research Quarterly*, vol. 16, pp. 219–228, London 1965.

Berry, B. and G. Barnum, Aggregate relations and elemental components of central place systems, *Journal of Regional Science*, vol. 4, pp. 35–68, Philadelphia 1962.

Bos, H. C., *Spatial dispersion of economic activity*, Rotterdam 1965.

Britton, N. H., The classification of cities: Evaluation of Q-mode factor analysis, *Regional and Urban Economics*, vol. 2, no 4, pp. 333–356, Amsterdam 1973.

Chamberlin, E., *The theory of monopolistic competition*, Cambridge 1938.

Christaller, W., *Central Places in southern Germany*, New Jersey 1966.

Clark, C., *Population growth and land use*, New York 1967.

Coase, R. H., The nature of the firm, *Economica*, New Series, vol. 4, pp. 386–405, London 1937.

Dantzig, *Linear programming and extension*, Princeton University Press 1963.

Edel, N., Land values and the cost of urban congestion, *Political economy of environment: Problems of method*, The Hague 1972.

Engwall. L., Inequalities of firm sizes in different economic systems, *Zeitschrift für Nationalökonomie*, vol. 32 pp. 449–460, Springer-Verlag 1972.

Goreux, L. M. and A. S. Manne (eds.), *Multi-level planning: case-studies in Mexico*, Amsterdam 1973.

Gunnarsson, J., Industristruktur och arbetsplatskontroll (Industrial structure and democracy at the plant of work) *Plan no 5*, Stockholm 1973.

Gunnarsson. J., R. Wigren and J. Wästlund, Problem vid resursallokering (Problems of Resource Allocation) memorandum no 36, Nationalekonomiska institutionen, Göteborg 1972.

Hadley, G., *Linear algebra*, Massachussets 1969.

Haran, E. G. P., and D. R. Vinning, A modified Yale-Simon model allowing for intercity migration and accounting for the observed form of the size distribution of cities, *Journal of Regional Science*, vol. 13, pp. 421–437, Philadelphia 1973.

Harman, H., *Modern factor analysis*, The University of Chicago Press 1960.

Hjalmarsson, L., The size distribution of establishments and firms derived from an optimal process of capacity expansion, *European Economic Review*, vol. 5, pp. 123–140, Amsterdam 1974.

Hotelling, H., Stability in competition, *Economic Journal*, vol. 39, pp. 41–57, London 1929.

Hymer, S., and P. Pashigan, The size and rate of growth, *Journal of Political Economy*, vol. 70, pp. 556–569, Chicago 1962.

Ijiri, Y., and H. I. Simon, Business firm growth and size, *American Economic Review*, vol. 54, pp. 77–89, Wisconsin 1964.

Intriligator, M. D., *Mathematical optimization and economic theory*, Prentice-Hall 1971.

Isard, W., *Location and space-economy*, The Massachusetts Institute of Technology 1956.

Johnson, B., and A. Meuller, Interaktioner mellan konsumtion och storstadstil lväxt (Interactions between Consumption and urban Growth), Department of Economics, Gothenburg, avhandling 1971.

Johnston, J., *Econometric methods*, New York 1972.

Jones, K. J., and C. J. Wyott, Toward a typology of American cities, *Journal of Regional Science*, vol. 10, no 2, pp. 217–224, Philadelphia 1970.

Kaldor, N., The equilibrium of the firm, *Economic Journal*, vol. 44, pp. 60–76, London 1934.

King, L. J., *Statistical analysis in geography*, Prentice-Hall 1969.

Koopmans, C., and M. Beckman, Assignment problems and the location of economic activities, *Econometrica*, vol. 25, pp. 53–75, New Haven 1957.

Koopmans, C., *Three essays on the state of economic science*, New York 1957.

Lamel, J., J., Richter and W. Teufelsbauer, Pattern of industrial structure and economic development, *European Economic Review*, vol. 3–1, pp. 47–64, Amsterdam 1972.

Lange, O., *Wholes and parts – a general theory of system behaviour*, Warszawa 1965.

Lange, O., *Introduction to economic cybernetics*, Warszawa 1970.

Lawley, D. N., and A. E. Maxwell, *Factor analysis as a statistical method*, London 1963.

Lefeber, L., *Allocation in space*, Amsterdam 1958.

Leibenstein, H., Allocative efficiency vs 'X-efficiency' *American Economic Review*, vol. 56, pp. 392–415, Wisconsin 1966.

Liljeström, R., *Uppväxtvillkor* (Conditions of Life during Infancy), Stockholm 1971.

Lösch, A., *The economics of location*, New Haven 1954.

Mansfield, E., Entry, Gibrat's law, innovation, and the growth of firms, *American Economic Review*, vol. 52, pp. 1023–1051, Wisconsin 1962.

Markowitz, H. M. and A. S. Manne, On the solution of discrete programming problems, *Econometrica*, vol. 25, pp. 84–110, New Haven 1957.

Mennes, L. B. M., J. Tinbergen and J. G. Waardenburg, *The element of space in development planning*, Amsterdam 1969.

Mennes, L. B. M., *Planning economic integration among developing countries*, Rotterdam 1973.

Mårdberg, B., *Dimensionsanalys för beteendevetare* (Factor Analysis for Behavioural Scientists), Stockholm 1969.

Parr, J. B. *Structure and size in the urban system of Lösch*, University of Pennsylvania 1973 (stencil).

Paelinck, J. H. and P. Nijkamp, *Operational theory and method in regional economies*, Fornborough 1975.

Ribrant, G., *Stordriftsfördelar inom industriproduktionen* (Economies of Scale in Manufacturing) SOU 1970:30, Stockholm 1970.

Richardson, H. W. *The economies of urban size*, Fornborough, Hants 1973a.

Richardson, H. W. Theory of the distribution of city sizes: Review and prospects, *Regional Studies*, vol. 7, pp. 239–251, New York 1973b.

Robinson, A., The problem of management and the size of firms, *Economic Journal*, vol. 44, pp. 242–257, London 1934.

Roepke, H., D. Adamus and R. Wiseman, A new approach to the identification of industrial complexes using input–output data, *Journal of Regional Science*, vol. 14, pp. 15–29, Philadelphia 1974.

Serck-Hanssen, J., *Some mathematical models on the spatial dispersion of industry*, Netherlands economic institute, memo 1961.

Serck-Hanssen, J., *Optimal Patterns of Location*, Amsterdam 1970.

Silberston, A., Economies of scale in theory and practice, *The Economic Journal*, vol. 82, pp. 369–391, London 1972.

Simon, H, On a class of skewed distribution, *Biometrika nr 42*, vol. 42, pp. 425–439, 1955.

Simon, H. A. and C. P. Bonini The size distribution of business firms, *American Economic Review*, vol. 48, pp. 607–617, Wisconsin 1958.

Simpson, D. and J. Tsukui The fundamental structure of input–output tables *The Review of Economics and Statistics*, vol. 47, no 4, pp. 434–446, Cambridge Massachusetts 1965.

Singer, H. W., The 'Courbe des populations '; Aparallel to Pareto's law,*The Economic Journal*, vol. 46, pp. 254–263, London 1936.

Smithies, A., Optimum location in spatial competition, *Journal of Political Economy*, vol. 49, pp. 423–439, Chicago 1941.

Snickars, F., *Convexity and duality properties of a quadratic intraregional location model*, Department of mathematics, Royal Institute of Technology, Stockholm 1973 (stencil). SOU 1971:75

Stuart, C., *Search and the organization of market places*, Malmö 1975.

Tinbergen, J., The hierarchy model of the size distribution of centres, *Regional Science Association*, vol. 20, pp. 65–68, Philadelphia 1967a.

Tinbergen, J., *Development planning*, London 1967b.

Tinbergen, J., Some thoughts on mature socialism, *Studies in economic planning over space and time*, Judge, G. S., Takayama, T. (ed), Amsterdam 1973.

Vanek, J., *The general theory of labor managed market economics*, Cornell University 1970.

Ward, B., City structure and interdependence, *Regional Science Association*, vol. 10, pp. 207–221, Philadelphia 1963.

Yasida, K., *Lectures in differential and integral equations*, Interscience 1960.

Zipf, G. K., *Human behavior and the principle of least effort*, Cambridge, Massachusetts 1949.

Studies in applied regional science

Vol. 1
On the use of input-output models for regional planning
W. A. Schaffer

This volume is devoted to the use of input-output techniques in regional planning. The study provides a clear
introduction to the essential ideas of input-output analysis.
Particular emphasis is placed on the intricate problems of
data collection at a regional level.
Attention is focused on the applicability of input-output
analysis in the field of regional planning. Alternative
methods such as shift-and-share techniques are discussed.
For means of clear illustration an extensive regional study
of the Georgia economy has been capably employed.

ISBN 90 207 0626 8

Vol. 2
Forecasting transportation impacts upon land use
P. F. Wendt

This reader concentrates on transportation problems in
urban areas. After a survey of model techniques for
analyzing transportation and land use problems, several
new methods in the field of transportation and land-use
planning (including Delphi-methods and interaction
models) are developed. In the study particular attention
is paid to forecasting techniques for regional-urban deve-
lopments. The book is exemplified by an extensive set of
applied methods in transportation land-use planning for
the Georgia region.

ISBN 90 207 0627 6

Martinus Nijhoff Social Sciences Division

Vol. 3
Estimation of stochastic input-output models
S. D. Gerking

The primary objective of this monograph is to develop a method for measuring the uncertainty in estimates of the technical coefficients in an input-output model. Specifically, it is demonstrated that if two-stage least squares is used to estimate these parameters, then uncertainty may be judged according to the magnitude of the standard errors of these estimates.

This study also describes three further applications of the two-stage least squares estimation technique in an input-output context. The techniques and applications are illustrated using cross-sectional input-output data from West Virginia.

ISBN 90 207 0628 4

Vol. 4
Locational behavior in manufacturing industries
William R. Latham III

Agglomerative economies form a central concept in regional science. Yet an empirical determination of agglomeration advantages has been minimal up to now. To help remedy the situation, this study contains an effort to gauge the order of magnitude of agglomeration advantages, based on a careful inspection of industrial location data. The determinants of geographic association behavior by individual industry are carefully analysed. A statistical test shows that general agglomerative economies are significant factors for industrial location behavior. The result of the study, and the policy conclusions it would seem to justify, are presented; moreover, ways of extending and improving the analysis are suggested.

ISBN 90 207 0638 1

Vol. 5
Regional economic structure and environmental pollution
B.E.M.G. Coupé
This book deals with the ever-increasing problem of
pollution. The author has constructed an extensive
interregional model for economic activities and pollution.
Each region has its own internal structure, expressed by
means of intersectoral commodity flows, investments,
employment, consumption and pollution. In addition,
interregional linkages are taken into account.
Coupé's two-region model (applied to some Dutch
provinces) is used to calculate an equilibrium in terms
of production and pollution abatement. The solution
procedure is based on a programming model. The model
aims at supplying a means of fighting pollution and
managing the environment, with a view to guiding the
regions to an acceptable life level.

ISBN 90 207 0646 2

Vol. 6
The demand for urban water
P. Darr, S. L. Feldman, C. Kamen
Because the urban water industry remained relatively
impervious to veneral inflationary trends until the early
1970's tariff design and water demand forecasting played
a relatively minor role in utility management. General
shortages in supply were often abetted by capacity
additions designed using common engineering practice.
However, the range of choice for water management can
include adjustments to remedy disequilibria through
management of the demand side of the market.
This volume explores the components affecting demands
using combined economic, engineering and social
psychological tools and recommends remedies in tariff
design to conform to basic economic postulates.

ISBN 90 207 0647 0